SECOND INNINGS

On men, mental health and cricket

First published 2021 by
FREMANTLE PRESS

Fremantle Press Inc. trading as Fremantle Press
25 Quarry Street, Fremantle WA 6160
(PO Box 158, North Fremantle WA 6159)
www.fremantlepress.com.au

Cover images: Alessandro Bogliari, unsplash.com;
Kimbomac, shutterstock.com
Printed by McPherson's Printing, Victoria, Australia.

 A catalogue record for this
book is available from the
National Library of Australia

ISBN 9781925816440 (paperback)
ISBN 9781925816457 (ebook)

 Department of
Local Government, Sport
and Cultural Industries

Fremantle Press is supported by the State Government through
the Department of Local Government, Sport and Cultural Industries.

Publication of this title was assisted by the Commonwealth Government through
the Australia Council, its arts funding and advisory body.

MIX
Paper from
responsible sources
FSC® C001695

SECOND INNINGS

On men, mental health
and cricket

BARRY NICHOLLS

FREMANTLE PRESS

Barry Nicholls is a journalist and broadcaster who has written nine books including *For Those Who Wait: The Barry Jarman Story* and *You Only Get One Innings: Family, Mates and the Wisdom of Cricket*. Barry has broadcast on the ABC for close to two decades, including presenting a sports books podcast for ABC Grandstand for five years. He lives in Perth with his partner Ann and their four children.

This book is dedicated to my children Jacy, Ambrose, Harry and Ellie to show that there is always a road back no matter how rough life gets.

It is in remembrance of my father, Leslie Albert Nicholls (1927–2019), and an acknowledgement of my mother, Margaret Elaine Nicholls. Both have been warriors through time for me, and both are much loved.

It is also for the underestimated. Stay that way and you will always surprise.

AUTHOR'S NOTE

This is my story as I remember the events outlined and passed down.

> The present as Frost puts it,
> Is too much for the senses
> Too crowded, too confusing
> Too present to imagine
>
> – Roger Khan, *The Boys of Summer*

CONTENTS

Prologue

It was my Greg Chappell moment. Not his immaculate 131 in the Second Test at Lord's in 1972, walking off to a standing ovation from MCC Members. Or the twin tons against the West Indies at the Gabba in 1975/76. Not even his final 182 against Pakistan at the SCG in early January 1984.

My Greg Chappell moment was like his extended run of ducks in 1981/82. Seven ducks, four in a row in fifteen internationals. This was the bearded, jumpy Chappell in the Australian helmet with temple guards, no front visor. It was the only time he lost his confident swagger. Chappell looked like he'd rather be anywhere but out in the middle. Not that I could blame him. Repeatedly facing 'the four horsemen of the apocalypse' must have been a disillusioning task. Holding, Roberts, Croft, Garner.

And then there were more. Marshall, Davis, Patterson. The West Indian bowlers were relentless. Whistle 'em around your ears at 100 miles per hour. And sometimes on ill-prepared wickets. Like the MCG, where the ball kept low one moment and sailed over your head the next. Greg Chappell's run of ducks. That was me from June 2014 to May 2016. Not one delivery in my half of the pitch. Or at least it felt that way.

Ducking and weaving. Tumbling onto my backside. Not really watching the ball.

I use cricket's language and references to describe life. But let me introduce myself. My name is Barry, middle name Milton, as Dad's nod to the famous poet. Growing up, I knew nothing about *Paradise Lost*. All I knew was that Milton the Monster was a character in a 1970s cartoon, and I never filled out my full name on school forms. It was too embarrassing. Still, my cricketing mates called me Milt.

I'm a generation Xer or a cusp baby boomer, depending on which guide you use. A cricket tragic; although I can bowl better off spinners than the former prime minister John Howard in Pakistan 2004 (look it up on YouTube).

My heroes were Ian Chappell, Dennis Lillee, Rod Marsh and Kim Hughes (Three-Tester Wally Edwards for a while but let's limit it to longevity in the game for simplicity.) Full of macho and bravado. Moustaches, long hair and open-chested shirts. Real men didn't cry – until Kim Hughes broke that duck, when he resigned the captaincy against the West Indies and was pilloried across the country.

'Don't cry like a girl,' was a schoolyard taunt if anyone broke down in tears. Aussie cricketers were considered real men. 'Men's men'. That's what I wanted to be. A man's man. Someone who was tough and led by example. Who never backed down or showed any sign of real emotion. Real men always showed up. They drank beer. Sometimes lots of it. The more you drank, the more of a man you were. My dad, Les, was the exception to this rule. He rarely drank. But he was a man's man in other ways.

I grew up in the 1970s, a much different time to now. Gender identity was clear. No unisex toilets. That would have given 1970s mothers a heart attack. No talk of LGBTQI or binary and non-binary sexuality either. Things were straightforward, or at least they seemed to be. In 2013 I wrote *You Only Get One Innings: Family, Mates and the Wisdom of Cricket*, a story of recollections about what cricket had taught me. But that was only part of the story. What followed started on a slow burn. I was like one of those plots of land with a fifty-year fuel load on a forty-degree day with 100 km/h winds. Just one small spark was all that was needed.

In the ensuing years, there were times I felt so bereft I'd scope out trees on my daily drive to work from Busselton to Bunbury. On average, at least six men in Australia kill themselves every day. Every day six families, friends and communities shatter as a life disappears. Some never find their way out. But eventually I got lucky. Two great doctors helped guide me to the light, and the overriding emotion is one of gratitude. Here's the story.

1. August 2014

The light reflects off metal palings as I pull my car into the hospital grounds. The park is close to full. I negotiate wire fences strewn with orange-coloured plastic and settle on a makeshift area near construction work. Men in hard hats with bored gazes try to look busy. Rather than walking down the beach, I'm soon staring at a slightly off-white wall in the new Busselton hospital. That's me on the red-covered nylon chair. Intent on my mobile phone.

A corkboard of pamphlets. Signs like *Don't mix alcohol with medication* watch on. I did it like everybody else. Walked in the hospital door, turned left past the physiotherapy unit, and then three quick steps toward where I'm going. Said my name.

The receptionist smiled without judgement. 'Thanks Barry, take a seat.'

It's quiet. People rarely raise their voices. All whispers. I dare not look up, in case I see someone I know. It's a small country town. Everyone knows everyone.

A young bloke in his twenties across from me can barely remain still. He's curly-haired, a bit wide-eyed and strung out. Like I used to be before I opened the batting against the new ball. He scrapes his feet forwards and backwards. Like he has paintbrushes on them, colouring the floor.

I feel even more alone. He jolts up like an electric shock, and walks.

Does a lap of a small waiting area and sits again. Like a choreographed movement. His dad moves next to him and holds him gently by the arm, whispering into his ear. It doesn't make much difference. He's jiggling his legs, sighing, his diaphragm slowly moving up and down. Up and down in a sea of pain.

I try to stay composed but I'm *jumpy as*. I'll jump at anything. A bearded doctor with a serious expression opens the door a few metres to my left. He greets the young man. 'Come in please.'

The young patient walks with his head bowed through the door. Like he is defeated. I wonder what his story is. We all have stories, a series of highs and lows. Some are more extreme than others. How things can quickly change. A year ago, life was great. I'd just published a popular and well-received book, I was at the top of my game broadcasting, and family life was great. I seemed to have limitless energy, juggling numerous challenges with ease. But now here I am. Sitting and waiting. To see a man called Dr Fabrizio Goria. Despite the publicity about a lack of mental health access, I get an appointment straight away. A door opens to my left and Dr Goria, a tall, lean psychiatrist in his early forties, pokes his head around the corner.

'Hello, how are you today, Barry?' His approach is informal and friendly. His smile is reassuring.

I nod and follow him into a room with two chairs and a small table. I'm here for him to check medications.

Dr Goria again explains about the serotonin levels in the brain, the feel-good transmitter. The way my mind has been caught in a loop of worry, like there's no off switch. The thoughts keep being recycled, which just intensifies anxiety.

'This may take a little while, but we need to find the sweet spot with the medication that's right for you.'

Sweet spot. That's a cricketing term. As Dr Goria gets to know me, he occasionally throws in a sporting metaphor to keep me at ease.

But there's no respite. Just like Greg Chappell in the early 1980s.

Deep down, I know I just need to watch each ball carefully. Once I start middling a few, I'll be through this and into my next innings.

And that is ultimately how it turns out, but it will take some time and a whole lot of pain.

And help.

Dust sprays into the sunlight as a thousand memories launch.

The plastic container opens with a creaking sound. Motes rise and magazines fall over the side. I'm in the shed going through old cricket magazines. Found one from around 1982, more broadsheet than magazine. I can't remember the publication, but it was short-lived.

My eyes track to a story about a player who arrives at the ground only to discover he's lost his car keys. He starts to panic. All he can think about is how he's going to find them. His captain wins the toss and he pads up to open the batting against the new ball. He's still wondering what happened to his keys and what he will have to do if he can't find them. His anxiety intensifies. He's lost the ability to think in the present. Like me when it all started in June 2014. Or maybe that's just when I think it began.

Fiddle with the top of the pad, flick the collar and grab the box. Just like Ian Chappell did and Steve Smith now does. A series of nervous tics. Sometimes called OCD, though it's not. It's a controlled ritualised habit. Scratch my sprigs on the crease. Adopt the batting stance, look up and lightly tap the bat on the ground. The opening bowler prepares to run in. Fielders who have been constantly chirping fall silent. The internal monologue 'lift the bat early and get your feet moving' fades as the umpire calls 'play'.

Cricket and anxiety go together like a hand in a glove. Perhaps that's part of the allure. A game that encourages in small doses and punishes in large measure.

One mistake and you spend the rest of the day watching team mates score the runs you should have. The uncertainty and injustices appeal, doubly so because I am one of a subset of cricketer. I am an opening batsman.

I face the new ball that's hard and shiny and swings. Part of me relishes the challenge. The other part hates it. Facing the quicks, you need to react in an instant. Like you have been trained to in all those net sessions. Sometimes you go into bat after spending most of the day in the field. Knowing it is just long enough to get out but not enough time to make a score.

Cricket's always keeping you in check, making sure you don't get ahead of yourself. Worry is at the heart of the game and many of those who play it. But I have an anxiety that can change gears rapidly from zero to 100 in a few seconds. It also makes me vigilant. To be the best I can be. Some days it turns against me. Today is one of those days. Like a spell has been cast.

I am driving the monotonous stretch of road that is Bussell Highway to Bunbury. Past the small town of Capel on the right, and later the outlying Bunbury suburb of Dalyellup. The same journey. Every day for seven years. Boredom only accentuated by rain and darkened skies in winter.

I listen to talk on the radio. Let it wash over me, half listening, half not. Blah, blah, blah, like a sermon from the mount. Talkback callers spill in with their opinions. Occasionally there is a personal story. My ears prick up. A man on a disability pension speaks. It's a few days after the State Budget and utilities are on the rise again.

'I won't have enough money to heat my house this winter. I'll have to wear three layers of clothing to bed.'

The scenery drifts by. I used to be surprised at the greenery and the lushness of the trees and surrounds. Fresh from Alice Springs, where it was all heat, red dirt and blaring blue skies. It rarely rained, but when it did the Todd River ran and green sprouts rose from the desert sands.

Each day I stare straight ahead with my hands firmly on the steering wheel. I feel like a statue.

Then I don't.

A white four-wheel drive jags off the straight and narrow toward me. Like a shark in the water swiftly changing direction.

I brake. Swing my car hard left onto the gravel. My hands on the steering wheel bounce up and down. I veer away from the road toward a farm fence and stop. Almost a head-on.

That's how quickly it can happen. Like an unplayable ball in a game of cricket. I look in the rear-vision mirror and gradually ease my way back onto the highway.

At lunchtime I go for a walk through a typical suburban shopping plaza. Target, Kmart, cafes and mobile-phone shops fill the centre. Mums with toddlers and aged pensioners have cups of coffee and share stories. It's an encapsulation of modest suburbia where consumerism is king. I'm no different. A discounted Michael Jordan biography sits under my arm.

I'm just through the glass sliding doors. A cold breeze blows, the sort where you wonder if you should be wearing a jumper. My mobile phone rings. My nerves start to jangle in an almost synchronised manner.

'Hello.' I'm talking in that urgent 'let this not be the doctor' kind of way.

'Is that Mr Nicholls?'

'Yes, it is.'

'The doctor would like you to come and see him about your test results.'

'Is it urgent?'

'The doctor would like you to come in and see him about the test results,' she repeats.

I hang up and walk in an uncertain anxious fog. Worst-case scenario? Of course, it is. I feel like Woody Allen's alter ego who's constantly on the lookout for a tumour.

We all have buttons. Buttons can be pushed.

2. Some of life's complexities · 1940s/1970s

It's buried on page five of the newspaper. Just a few lines.

It's quietly, quietly as she goes. The US B-29 bomber *Enola Gay* has dropped the first atom bomb on Hiroshima. The force is felt more than a marathon away. Nearly 150,000 blown away, every building for miles obliterated.

Dad celebrates his eighteenth birthday on 9 August, 1945, when they drop the second one on Nagasaki. Forty thousand killed instantly, double that number eventually lost. Six days later the Japanese surrender. It is front page news then.

Dad never reports for training.

'They knew I was coming,' he says.

He doesn't intend to be flippant about such hideous events, just knows how lucky he was.

'My bones could have been rotting on some Pacific Island.'

Sliding doors.

Dad's brother Uncle Bob, two years older, works for the Railways during the war. Misses the action. It is a burden he carries his entire life. Bob wanted to join up but Cecil, my grandfather, a Great War veteran, won't let him. Not until Bob was twenty-one. But by then it is all over. Cecil gives him a piano as solace. The piano is rarely played.

By the late 1970s, Bob has turned fifty. He is a stickler for turning up to work each day, in charge of seventy people, helping the trains run on time. But into his fifties, he loses weight, can barely raise a conversation, and becomes reliant on his wife, my Auntie Irene. Bob ages considerably overnight. He tries going back to work for a while but is off the pace. He lives his remaining days on a pension, barely able to answer a question with more than one word.

Well, that's how I remember him. Was it depression? No one knew or would say. You didn't talk about depression in the 1970s.

When the rubber hits the road for me in 2016, I think of Bob. Maybe I've received 'an unplayable ball' at fifty-one and will never hit the ball off the square again.

My mum Margaret Blight grows up on a wheat and sheep farm outside of Waikerie, a small town 100 or so miles from Adelaide. The Riverland is also citrus country. And it's dry. The farms were established under the Soldier Land Settlement Scheme after the Great War.

When the thermometer tips 100 degrees Fahrenheit, Mum and her older brother Geoff sneak away to the banks of the Murray River, swinging off the rope and launching themselves into the dark, cool waters.

Mum rides a horse to Moorook West Primary, a small one-teacher school, a six-and-a-half-mile return trip. Prisoners at the Japanese internment camp run toward her when they see the little girl on the horse approaching. She eventually takes another route to avoid scaring the horse, although I suspect her parents tell her to for other reasons.

Riding to school is part of daily farm life, with chores like milking the cows and moving the sheep between the River farm nearby at Lowbank and the Holder Siding farm on the train line from Waikerie to Karoonda.

Some days Margaret's mother Elsie buys food and other goods from a paddle steamer; in exchange her dad Billy supplies wood to fuel the boat.

There is no electricity, indoor plumbing or running water, no nearby shops or phone. The nearest town is a bum-numbing, sixteen-mile drive on the back of the buckboard, often over sand drifts and obliterated fence posts.

Inside the house, a large black urn sits on top of the stove, supplying hot water for plates, cups and bath water. Nanna Blight also makes bread, and feeds the farm workers, the pigs and chickens. She renders the extra animal fat to create soap and candles, looks after the vegetable garden, collects the eggs for market and carefully cleans the kerosene glasses for lighting, making sure she doesn't break fragile filaments or spill any kero.

Mum's dad Billy Blight helps organise the workers. Huge draught horses pull the plough, while hands shovel wheat into the winnower, which runs into a bag supported by an iron trolley. Whenever a dust storm sweeps through, wet paper is scattered on the floor to absorb the mess.

By the late 1940s, Europe is recovering from the scorched-earth policy of the Second World War. The price of wheat goes sky high. The Korean War later dramatically pushes up the price of wool. Better than average rainfall means that for a while the good times roll. Mum and Geoff are sent to boarding schools in Adelaide. A big new American sedan arrives on the farm. A few years later Nanna takes a well-deserved rest and cruises to England, visiting relatives in Hull. But good times never last.

Mum's dad Billy Blight has three children from his first marriage to Margaret (Maggie). It is a shotgun wedding in July 1909. Along comes Amy, Billy Junior and then Ambrose. Maggie dies of typhoid in December 1915, six months after Billy departs for The Great War. Billy might have been glad to get away. His wife's sister, Georgina, who lived with Billy and Maggie, is pregnant with his child when he goes.

Billy is part of the 32nd Battalion that fought on the Western Front. They sail on 18 November 1915 on the HMAT A2 *Geelong*. The battalion travels from Alexandria to Egypt for training next to the pyramids and then a crowded train journey to Marseille in southern France. From there they are transported to the front.

Three days later they are slaughtered in the mud and the mind-rattling noise of constant shelling. There are 718 casualties – ninety percent of the battalion. Billy is hit in the hip and lungs but somehow survives. The battalion is sent to the front again. By September 1917, they are in Belgium. My grandfather is incapacitated. This time it's shell shock.

During leave in Cornwall for two weeks, he gets engaged to one of his second cousins. Then he leaves for Australia. Burns his bridges. Billy is shipped to Melbourne, then by rail to Adelaide.

Billy meets my nanna, Elsie Wilkinson-Watkinson, walking along the beach at Taperoo where they'd been demobbing.

Elsie's dad was a pub owner in Hull who brought his eleven kids to Australia to get away from his second wife. She followed them out anyway. But Elsie's dad took up with his younger housekeeper, Greta. As a young girl, Margaret used to catch them in bed when she stayed over.

Billy might have smiled at all this, but he's just been diagnosed with a precursor to tuberculosis. He isn't the only one, coming from the wet conditions of the trenches. He thinks he will move to a dryer climate. Also, away from Penola in the south-east. And the scandal of his first wife's sister.

After Billy marries Elsie, they take up a farm in Waikerie, surrounded by German immigrants from the early 1900s.

Life is far from smooth sailing.

Billy's kids eventually return home. The two boys, Billy Junior and Ambrose, struggle to connect with their father in any meaningful way. Amy is treated more like a maid than a daughter.

In the photo, Ambrose sits in the front row of the 1935 Polwarth Football League premiers, a member of the Birregurra football team. He's twenty-one and built like a brick outhouse. Ambrose has been living and working with his older brother Billy as a labourer in the Otway Ranges.

He is a handy cricketer too. Ambrose once takes six for forty for the small SA town eighty miles north-east of Adelaide, Blanchetown against Ramco, five bowled, including two Darlings, relations of former Test captain Joe Darling.

In 1940, he trains as a chalkie in Adelaide before being posted to a one-teacher school at Woods Flat near Morgan in South Australia.

He isn't going to enlist, but Billy Senior thinks it a good idea.

He says Ambrose should do 'his bit', so he enlists in the air force in 1942.

As a little girl, my mum Margaret is close to her stepsister Amy. Puts her head on Amy's shoulder. Amy is more like a mum than her own. Amy marries Edgar and moves to his fruit block near Ramco where my mum goes for sleepovers. But Amy of the gentle touch dies of consumption in 1941 in the Waikerie hospital and is buried in the Ramco Cemetery.

'Here you go, shove this in your pocket.'

Mum takes the penny as a keepsake. It's the last thing Ambrose does before he leaves for interstate.

Patricia's the flame-haired girl who catches his attention in Sydney. He has a girlfriend in Morgan near Waikerie, but he marries Patricia anyway, on his way to becoming a navigator on a Lancaster bomber, flying missions over Germany. On August 24, 1942, he sets sail on the troop ship *Westernland*, arriving in England three months later. Flight training takes Ambrose to most corners of England and to Scotland.

He can read maps well and is transferred to Litchfield to crew up – it is the place where crews come together through word of mouth.

A letter home describes a bus trip to Cornwall, through twisted and narrow streets, its gutted churches 'roofless and gaping' where German bombs have struck.

In England's south-west, Ambrose tries to rebuild broken family connections. He meets May, the cousin Billy jilted all those years before. Ambrose even takes his own wedding photos from Sydney to show.

Flight training restarts with an urgency not seen before. There are simulated night fighter attacks escaping from searchlight combing. The fatigue, freezing cold and airsickness are just a hint of what was to follow.

In June 1943, the crew receives an above-average rating and is assigned to a four-engine Wellington at No. 466 Squadron, Leconfield. At the urging of the crew, dissatisfied that their plane has been superseded by the Lancaster, the pilot Stan Ireland meets his superiors at Australia House and challenges the assignment.

Soon they are doing three-week conversion training on Lancasters at RAF Lindholme in Yorkshire. Lancasters carry fire bombs, more than a thousand four-pounders, as well as special incendiaries including 56 thirty-pounders. Their job is delivering death. Also on board is a powerful enough cookie to burst open blocks of flats to clear the way.

Roll the dice. Thirty missions for the Aussies and Brits. Twenty-five for the Yanks. Bomber Command loses more than fifty percent. Eight missions is the average before you are toast.

The crew's first bombing mission to Nürnberg is uneventful despite an equipment failure and an unscheduled landing to refuel.

Missions take seven and a half hours, most of those terrifying. They bomb Mannheim, Hannover, Bochum, Hagen, Ludwigshafen, Kassel, Modane and Munich.

Ambrose is a prolific letter writer. After a raid on Munich on September 30, 1943, he writes:

> ... as we approached [the target] we were coned by searchlights and had to do very violent evasive action ... after three or four minutes we were out of them ... to

be caught in searchlights, worse still to be coned, and particularly over the target is fatal.

We could have dropped our bombs at random and scrammed, but no – we straightened up for our bombing run and as we did so, we were attacked by a fighter who fired a burst into us before we knew anything, we felt the hit, the plane shuddered, and we smelt the acid smell of the smoke and cordite in our nostrils.

The raid on Leipzig fails. Their oxygen masks malfunction and then they encounter a storm they cannot avoid. Engines stall and Ambrose writes that the plane 'dropped out of the sky like a log'. They limp home mostly avoiding flak as they cross the international border. Two engines fail. 'What a relief to be back. I cannot describe the tense feeling at the time, or the great feeling of relief and flatness on return.'

Eighteen missions down. Over 130 days, an average of one a week, but for a brief period they fly every second night.

On a cold, clear December 29, 1943, Ambrose is part of the crew of a Lancaster III JB-607 (AR-N) bomber nicknamed *Leader*. She takes off for Berlin on her nineteenth mission with seven crew on board. *Leader* is one of twenty-four aircraft departing from Binbrook. They leave just after 5pm.

They are nearing home when they begin to relax. The crew talk about what they'll do when they are out of this shithole and back in Australia.

They're over the border into Holland when a German Messerschmitt Bf 110G night fighter finds them.

Four are mortally wounded. The plane explodes and crashes

into a garden of a monastery in Bleijerheide near Kerkrade. The wreckage spreads to a nearby football pitch. Monks join the local Brandweer, the Dutch fire department, to douse the flames.

Only one crew member survives: twenty-two-year-old flight engineer air bomber Frank Seery. He jumps out as the pilot puts the plane in a spiral and is captured and held as a POW for the remainder of the war.

January 1944. It's a hot summer's day early in the new year. Nanna Blight prepares lunch, wiping the beads of sweat from her brow with her forearms. The family gathers in the lounge room of the Holder Siding farm.

Geoff, the apple of his mother's eye, is chipper. He has just rowed in the Head of the River. Geoff is also a boxer, a prefect, a swimmer and a lieutenant in the cadets at Scotch College.

Billy is standing in the kitchen stretching, after a morning mending fences.

There is a knock at the door.

'Deeply regret to inform that your son Ambrose Edward Blight...'

Billy struggles to stay on his feet. He weeps in his armchair.

It is the only time my mum sees her dad cry.

In the fog of war, false news circulates. Ambrose and some of the crew have been shot down while trying to parachute, a helpless way to die.

Billy carries that image of his son's death with him until a decade later, when he is his mid-sixties and he drops dead walking out the front door. Through the window, Elsie sees him fall, and she drops the dishes in the kitchen.

3. Vera and Cecil · 2014/1950s–1960s

My head hits the pillow. 'Tomorrow is another day,' says my GP, Tony Best. It becomes my mantra. I nod off easily. A deep sleep. Like disappearing into a black hole. Then I wake. Always at 3am. The alarm clock on the bedside table blinks at me. Pictures flicker through my mind. Like one of those disjointed reel-to-reel movies.

Images come and go. One night it's my family living in England in the 1960s; another it's our house at Lascelles Avenue, Beaumont, a decade later.

Then the mullet hairstyles, the light fading at the Kensington District Cricket Club in the 1980s. Beers and talk of girls.

Some images stay. An old colour photo of my paternal grandparents, Vera and Cecil Nicholls.

It's the 1950s. Vera's wearing a straw hat and a blue and white flowered dress. Cecil's in a dark jacket and white shirt. There's a shiny black Holden in the background. It gleams in the sun like my school shoes after Mum chips me about not putting enough Kiwi shoe shiner on them.

My parents stand next to Vera, Cecil and Bob, contrasting the generations. Mum wears a summer skirt. Dad stands with a camera draped around his bare chest next to his brother. They display the brashness of youth. The twenty-somethings. The 'we're coming through and nothing's going to stop us' look. But Vera wears a cheeky grin. Like she knows something the rest of us don't. Maybe it's her lucky streak in winning competitions. She'd been born on the third day of the third month of 1893 and lives her life believing there's something special about the number three.

Years later Gran will win our family a doghouse worth $333. Gran needed some luck. When she was a teenager she lost her dad to Bright's disease.

The family believe it is an 'act of God'. Her mum Addie (Adelaide) Crowder with almond-shaped eyes plays the piano at dances to pay the bills and support Vera and her five siblings.

Vera is an eastern-suburbs girl from Adelaide. Parkside is a well-heeled part of town and she grows up as a sociable, happy child with a supportive extended family.

She meets Cecil. I don't know where but he's working-class through and through. Vera thinks their engagement will never end. But when it does, Cecil provides a roof over their heads during the Depression, when many couldn't, a 'gentleman's villa' at 42 Ebor Avenue, Mile End.

Cecil had his own loss. His dad, Edwin, did a runner to the Western Australian goldfields in 1894, abandoning his wife Sarah and their four young boys. Edwin never came back and was buried in an unmarked grave near Coolgardie.

Sarah returned to work as a seamstress while her sons left school early to work in their grandfather Wilmshurst's general store in North Adelaide.

On May 26, 1900, Cecil received a Bible for his eighth birth-day. It was signed *To Dear Cecil With love from His affectionate*

Grandmother. There was family support but the boys rarely socialised, aware of the stigma of having a deserting father.

When Sarah became ill, Cecil paid his mum's bills on a railway worker's wages. Life was a serious business for a young man before he even went to war.

Later, whenever Dad hears the song 'Mr Bojangles', he shows rare signs of emotion. It reminds him of his dad, Cecil, although he won't tell me why. But my father always plays his cards close to his chest, even to his sons.

Cecil Nicholls survives the blood-soaked French trenches for close to two years. Two years in the mud, stink and death of the war. In December 1916 alone, British casualties pass 400,000 in the battles of Ypres, Passchendaele and Messines. Cecil sends letters to Vera back home at 34 Stamford Street, Parkside, South Australia. One is a postcard labelled 'A Kiss from France' with a floral decoration on the cover. In the top right-hand corner are the words 'On Active Service'. Cecil has written: 'I had leave today and visited a small town 1 ½ miles distant. The fruit here is lovely but very expensive.'

Packages of books addressed to Cecil arrive. The sender is his cousin Roy Wilmshurst. But Cecil doesn't have much time for reading books. His short, wiry physique makes him a runner which also means he is a priority target for enemy snipers. He eventually catches a bullet to the head.

Sliding doors.

Cecil's repatriated and when he arrives home, he has physically altered so much that his friends and family barely recognise him. He's also 'lost his edge' when it comes to playing his much loved footy.

During the Second World War, Cecil as a train driver helps transport the troops and equipment and is a largely absent father, spending his downtime quietly gardening. He can't stand noise. Not even the piano playing like he did when he was courting Vera.

'They were never the same as before the war,' Vera tells her sons.

Les and Bob hear the words 'shell shock' to explain their father's increasingly irritable behaviour.

Dad and my uncle Bob get out of the house as often as they can. Ride their bikes to the city's Palais Royal and the movies at the 'Thebbie' town hall.

Dad's studying at uni and teaching at the school he just left, while Bob soon leaves home to work with the South Australian Railways in Mt Gambier.

Polio and diphtheria epidemics sweep through Adelaide, adding another layer of worry. Ebor Avenue is not immune: one of Dad's schoolboy friends is hospitalised and returns months later wearing calipers.

There are some happy memories though, of annual summer holidays to Brighton, one of the work perks for Cecil. A free family tram trip where they enjoy a picnic basket, some ice-cream, and listen to a brass band. 'Smoke Gets in Your Eyes', from the musical *Roberta*, plays in the background. There's a cooling breeze while the family sit on a rug and chat as music fills the air.

It's dated January 23, 1957. The letter that tells it all but says nothing. From Cecil to Bob, written just weeks before Cecil bled to death in the chicken coop.

Dear Bob

We were glad to hear from you again to know you are well. We commence our 3 weeks leave on Mon Feb 4th ... Les, Margaret and family called tonight while we were having tea ... they are all well.

And then ...

Did you hear of that boy on a bike being killed by the train at Bowden, Bob? Well I was the driver. Look, Bob, it couldn't have been timed more exactly for the movies. The one train just cleared the crossing with flashing lights operating and me whistling and this poor boy came from behind the brake van and into the side of my engine. Bill Giddings fell in the pit at Mile End Loco this morning and suffered facial injuries, nothing very serious I believe. The weather has been wonderful, and a few plums are left and then the nectarines are almost ripe, to say nothing of the tomatoes. Mother has been busy preserving tomatoes and apricots.

Cecil is dying inside. But he can't, or doesn't want, to tell anyone.

He is instructed by Train Traffic Control to resume the journey before the mangled body of the child is cleared off the track, and Cecil is worried he'll go to jail. He later visits the boy's family despite Vera telling him not to.

The image of the boy's body haunts his dreams and reminds Cecil of what he'd seen on the Front. Prescribed antidepressants and tranquillisers, he dives further into depression.

When Cecil's cousin Roy Wilmshurst discovers Cecil in the chicken coop, he is still alive. An ambulance takes him to the Royal Adelaide Hospital, but Cecil is dead soon after.

Overwhelmed with grief and shock, Vera asks Roy to take the long drive to Salisbury to tell my dad the news and to have Les identify the body.

At the time of the accident, Cecil was sixty-four with forty-seven years of service. Under the circumstances, they could have easily pensioned him off rather than make him return to work.

It must have been horrible for Les, then only twenty-nine, with two small kids and a third on the way. I don't know if Dad ever got over it. Who would?

Cecil is later exonerated by the coroner's report. It will be another decade before the deputy commissioner of the SA branch of the Commonwealth Repatriation Department declares Cecil's death is attributable to his war service, finally allowing Vera to qualify for the War Widow Pension.

I find out about some of this when I am a teenager. Mum tells me in a fit of anger. But I am just the conduit. Her real target is Dad. Mum is annoyed because Dad isn't paying child support for 'the boy' as is stated in the lawyers' letters.

Words used as weapons. I don't know why Mum is so pissed off. She is the one who left Dad.

Vera is very canny, especially about money, and stays frugal after the Depression and the Second World War. Once she wins a competition from Adelaide's Radio station 5DN to help raise funds for the annual Christmas appeal.

December 27, 1949: headline: *Xmas Appeal nets 14,000 pounds*. The prize is a refrigerator. It is worth £119 – seven grand today – and spells the end of the icebox and regular visits to the corner deli to buy blocks of ice.

Her poem that bettered 10,000 entrants is as relevant now as it was then:

> When Children's Hospital bills fall due
> The payment is largely up to you
> So, dig down deep for your donation
> Bills can't be paid by admiration.

Her limerick is four lines, not five, but she still wins.

That final line is one that rolls down the years: *Bills can't be paid by admiration*. Dad remembers it almost seventy years later.

'Twenty-five, twenty-six, twenty-seven ...' I count the number of times I roll from side to side trying to get back to sleep.

Losing sleep kills you day by day. Reading used to help. I watch a DVD from a small portable player, and TV series like the English crime show *Broadchurch* and *The Fall*. I'm wide-awake and wired as the time 3:33 blinks back. Vera's looking down at me keeping an eye on things. She wouldn't be too happy with what she sees.

It'd remind her of the chicken coop.

Mum and Dad marry in January 1954, honeymooning with other couples at the Victorian coastal town of Lorne. The scientist and the nurse have three kids in four years without much support. There is no contraceptive pill in the 1950s. Other methods are unpopular with local doctors and pharmacists with religious affiliations. Australia was a different place back then.

My eldest brother Steve has a difficult start to life. The aftermath of a prolonged labour and his forceps delivery means Mum haemorrhages and has to go back to hospital for a month. She remembers floating above the bed and looking down. Mum never forgets the look of devastation on Steve's face when Nanna takes him back to Waikerie to look after while Mum recovers.

Mum should have married her childhood sweetheart. Geoff Blake was a handsome and curly-haired Waikerie carpenter who worked in the local mines. He wanted to travel overseas and move to Broken Hill where a 'lead bonus' would have doubled his wages. Mum didn't think it was such a good idea, not without her being there, at any rate. Geoff had a reputation as a 'bit of a lad about town' and I don't think Nanna approved.

By the early 1960s we are living at a Commonwealth rental house at Penfield Avenue, Salisbury North.

Geoff occasionally calls and drops off some fruit.

'How about we make a go of it?' he asks Mum.

'A bit late for that now,' she says, pointing to my three brothers.

Nanna hears a thundering noise from her house the day Geoff is blown up in a mining accident a few weeks later. A detonator has accidentally exploded.

On the cover of R.S. Whitington's *An Illustrated History of Australian Cricket,* Victor Trumper lunges from the popping crease. His front foot is elevated, the bat raised in baseball fashion. Yellow writing sits on a black background. A gloveless left hand guides control of the stroke.

Cricket books awaken me to stories and provide an escape from reality. I stare at the black and white photos and imagine

I'm back in time. Like *Field of Dreams*, the movie about the Chicago White Sox player 'Shoeless Joe' Jackson who helped throw the 1919 World Series. Kevin Costner plays the corn-farmer who built a baseball diamond to lure his dead heroes back for one last game to resolve his past.

My first glimpse of my family's history is through colour slides that complement tales from my three older brothers, Steve, John and Ralph – nine, seven and six years older.

For three and a half years Dad was seconded by the Royal Radar Establishment in the UK to liaise with the British Army and weapon contractors to work on the project ET-316, later designated *Rapier* – the plane killer that was first fired in anger during the Falklands War in 1982.

A photo sits on my desk that marks the beginning. My family is at Adelaide Airport to fly to Melbourne to catch the *Oriana* to England. There is a propeller plane lurking in the background. Dad looks excited like he can't wait to get on board. Mum, holding a toddler (me), looks more trepidatious. My brothers are dressed in suits; the eldest, Steve, with pursed lips, holds a camera.

We travel first class. It's manna from heaven for my parents. Mum finally gets a break from the grind of raising four young kids. Three weeks, through the Indian Ocean into the Red Sea toward Egypt and the Suez Canal and on to the Mediterranean. To Colombo, Aden, Cairo, Naples and finally Southampton. We sit on camels and see the pyramids of Giza on the banks of the Nile, then arrive in England on a bitterly cold winter's day in December 1964.

We spend six more weeks in a single room, holed up in the

castle-like Abbey Hotel in Malvern. Green shrubbery decorates the walls, like the hotel is growing a beard. There's snow and ice on the footpaths and icicles on the leaves. A shortage of family housing in the area means our weekend trips around the countryside to try to find a house to lease have been fruitless.

Then a favour is called in by Nanna Blight, which leads to Dad's 'High Tea' appointment with the Australian consulate to London, Alick Downer. He's a long-time friend of Billy Blight, who has strong masonic connections and used to read Hansard and urged his farm workers to do the same to understand how decisions in parliament were made.

After their meeting, the lease comes through for a two-storey house with a rolling backyard in Herefordshire. Hill Orchard has five bedrooms, each with a gas fire, and a coal-fired boiler in the kitchen to heat water for the background radiant heaters. Dad furbishes the place on hire purchase, a risky move in the 1960s with no credit cards and without his having a specified length of contract in England.

You take the road from Great Malvern, to a steepish climb, from either end through the Wyche Cutting along the side of the Malvern Hills. Toward our end, an S bend needs to be traversed. Our new house is near a small village called Colwall.

We've transitioned to all the comforts of middle-class in just one boat trip. My parents' marriage is invigorated and the trip shows how life moves in strange ways.

One Saturday afternoon on the narrow lanes, our Opel family station wagon collides with another car, cancelling our family trip to Scotland. No one is harmed, and instead we spend separate weeks touring Wales, Devon and Cornwall.

We've been in England just over one year when Dad prepares for his annual trip back to Australia. The month-long visit is to test the *Rapier* missile around the outback town of Woomera, 270 miles north of Adelaide, deep in the South Australian desert.

An order soon comes down for Les Nicholls to escort a bust of the deceased Sir Winston Churchill to Australia for the South Australian Parliament as a commemorative symbol of support.

Dad takes the Douglas DC-3 flight wearing a suit. The bust sits on the seat next to him the whole way. In January 1966, it takes forty-eight hours with multiple stops.

Mum is left to fend with four kids and a young female helper, in the cold of an English winter.

Dad spends three weeks in Woomera. He stays in primitive wooden huts with no air conditioning that are surrounded by dust, flies, heat and often fierce winds. The days are long with pre-dawn starts and evening finishes. But these are exciting times as mathematicians and scientists with windblown notes wait to see if their hard work has paid off.

An Ashes Test match is played at Adelaide Oval on the Australia Day long weekend. Dad and his workmates travel to watch a day of it. It is the Fourth Test of a five-match series with Australia, down one–nil leading into Adelaide. Shirtless men stand beneath the scoreboard drinking beers while Members in jackets and ties and women in fancy hats acknowledge on-field milestones with ripples of applause.

At night, cricket commentators' voices describing play from the other side of the world echo out of the radio in the lounge room at Hill Orchard, reminding us that Dad is far away but will be home soon.

Australia wins as Graham McKenzie takes six first-innings wickets. Australian openers Bob Simpson and Bill Lawry put on 244.

The day Dad returns, Mum keeps their door shut for him to recover. The sound of movement and the light leaking through the small opening finally indicate he is awake. We greet Dad with smiles and collect our presents.

The chill of an English winter turns young boys' ears red.

'Lick your finger and dab it against your ear. It works every time.'

Advice from my brothers on how to deal with hot ears is frequent.

I wonder why they are smiling.

Lick, wipe, lick, wipe. More frantic and more desperate with each wipe.

It lands me in trouble, one Sunday afternoon at the small local cinema near the foot of the Malvern Hills. I keep licking my finger. Mum keeps pushing it away.

A hush descends as the lights go out.

I stand up. 'Well what am I supposed to do with two bloody hot ears?' I yell.

Mum grabs my hand.

'I'll see you boys soon,' she hisses to the others.

Dad's peaceful afternoon in the shed is disturbed by our return.

Slides show young boys with baso haircuts, wing-nut ears and smiles as big as dinner plates.

'Smile.'

The camera captures the British Houses of Parliament, the Cotswolds, the Worcestershire cricket ground, the mountains in Switzerland on our trip around the Continent, and the red ears that accompany us everywhere.

The wharfies go on strike the week before we leave so we almost don't make it to Europe. Rearranged plans and airfreight save the day.

We cruise through the flat countryside of Belgium on a calm May evening with a sense of relief.

Then we stand on a scorching hot Italian summer's day in front of Rome's Trevi Fountain. Throw a coin with your right hand over your shoulder and it will land in the fountain. That's how close we are. Not like today, no rows of people lining up. Squinting at a Kodak camera bought in Ceylon on the way over, along with the expensive jewellery, Mum's rings and necklaces.

'C'mon Mum take the photo.'

'Stand still.'

'Smile.'

Click.

We break away like a cricket team back into the field after a drinks break.

Four boys line up ready to dive into a pool with a snow-capped mountain in the background. We ride chairlifts, take gondolas through the canals, walk art galleries, climb the Eiffel Tower and stare at cathedrals. We spend six weeks in a tent hired from the Malvern Boy Scouts.

There must have been some love in the marriage back then. And respect.

Fragments of memories eke out. Others spread like sand on a windy day, never to be reassembled in a logical form.

England wins the World Cup in the summer of 1966. A showery July day until the sun bursts through the heavens in the late afternoon. Kenneth Wolstenholme's now famous call – 'They think it's all over ... It is now' – as Geoff Hurst powers his third goal into the back of the net giving England a 4–2 win. The moment returns in colour images. England's bright red kit contrasts the white of Germany.

There is one name from England I remember, perhaps because it sounds different to other words. Aberfan.

October 1966: 116 children and 28 adults are killed when a slagheap, loosened by rain, slides its way down a hill and buries a school. I later read how one of the kids trapped by the deluge reached for a book lying on the floor, waiting for rescuers.

We had visited Wales not long before, marvelling at the thick Welsh accents, the rugged beaches and beauty of the countryside. Four boys sitting on a wire fence in Wales with a mining slagheap lurking ominously in the background. In the photo I'm pointing in the distance. The way kids do when they are learning to speak full sentences but can't quite yet put all the words together.

Aberfan becomes a symbol of horror. My parents utter that word like no other. They know what it represents.

When we return to Australia I am the only one in my class who has heard of the small Welsh town. Aberfan. Some nights the name appears in my dreams.

It's mid-1967 when we return to Australia after another four weeks of luxury on the *Oriana*. In our luggage sits a dinner menu. On its cover, a wandering albatross flies above a choppy ocean. Turn the page, and the lists of four-course meals and European wines are reminders of our time in England, an oasis in a desert of memories.

We stay temporarily in Blair Athol while, on a house block in Adelaide's eastern suburbs, a bulldozer carves out levels in the gully to create room for paths and a garden. Dad builds retaining walls and concrete paths. Then we move into 17 Lascelles Avenue in the foothills of Adelaide, a two-storey, five-bedroom, mansard-style house, Dutch colonial. The area is a reminder of Malvern and close to where Mum used to board at Presbyterian Girls College. Several streets in our new suburb of Beaumont are full of vacant blocks, but Lascelles only has one, at the tail-end of the avenue next to my friend Martin's house.

Weeds take hostage, making it harder to find any wayward tennis balls from cricket matches played against the wall that adjoins the asphalt court and makes a useful wicketkeeper and slips cordon.

Noise reverberates around the wooden floors of our house like thunder. It amplifies everything, including the growing sense of unease between my parents. Martin comes to play at my house but not that often.

We go for walks to the top of the street with my brown cocker spaniel, Snoopy, and Martin's dog, Bosca, before playing on the island, a mini triangular-shaped park across the road. We pause and look out on the city of Adelaide, down to the airport, and along the beaches and industrial suburbs of the north. We watch the planes fly across the sky and wish we were the ones going on a holiday.

Some days we drop in on Maria, a Greek lady who lives

halfway down the road in a small cream-brick house with her husband Bill, who was once a boxer. Bill is tall and skinny and often sits shirtless on a deckchair taking in the sun and drinking beer from a longneck on their back verandah. Maria, who must be close to sixty, has long dark black hair with flecks of grey. She wears lots of make-up and large gold chains. Some days I can't stop looking at the chains as they droop over her saggy bosoms. She serves up chilled glasses of lemonade to passing kids in the street.

When she speaks to you it feels like you are the only person in the world.

'Here you go love, and how are things at home?'

Stealthily she seeks out street gossip. Soft drinks are a rarity in our house, so I easily give up information in the way that kids being treated with such kindness sometimes do. If a family leaves the neighbourhood, Maria always knows why.

After twenty minutes or so she says, 'Don't be late, love, your mum will be getting worried.' She always has a huge smile as she waves you up the street.

4. Life isn't always just • 1970s

Genes guide the path. Mum is full of expression, sometimes with the effect of a mini cyclone; Dad keeps his feelings to himself but can silently seethe with anger before responding. If you push him too far he reacts in a way that makes you wish you hadn't. It is hard even at the best of times to know what he is feeling. Because of his work he lives in a world of secrets, and he is practised at not giving away too much. Only sometimes do I get a glimpse of this world.

Dad first takes me to the footy on Anzac Day 1970. Before the game, the crowds gathered at dawn. There were no mass audiences or patriotic jingoism, just veterans with grim faces walking with medals on their chest down King William Street through the city of Adelaide. Then later they got pissed in the surrounding pubs and played some two-up along the way.

A large group of anti–Vietnam War protestors fills the streets. We make our way to Adelaide Oval to watch the SANFL grand final replay between our team Sturt and Glenelg.

Dad parks near the Botanic Gardens and we stroll along North Terrace with the gathering crowd. We've just past the terraced apartments, the offices of the Campaign for Peace in Vietnam next to the Botanic Hotel, when a man descends the stairs.

'Hello Les.'

It's Brian Medlin, Dad's old mate from Adelaide Tech, and a lecturer at Flinders University. He's also involved in the Vietnam Moratorium Campaign, a national anti-war movement in Australia. They want troops withdrawn from Vietnam and a repeal of the National Service Act.

On the day of the footy Medlin looks intimidating. His generous and warm-spirited nature is hidden by a fearsome-looking black beard, moustache and a maniacal grin. He is standing in the smoke of a fire coming from the terraced apartments from where Medlin has descended.

They might be old friends, but Dad can't be seen with the leader of an anti-war movement. Les Nicholls works for the government helping design and test missiles. All the way with LBJ.

And now there are too many Australian soldiers returning in body bags and people are questioning Australia's involvement in this pointless war.

Medlin knows all about war. He had two brothers who were POWs in the Second World War. One died on the Burma Railway, the other survived Changi and became a leading academic. Dad even went to the coming-home party at the end of the war.

'Hello Les,' Medlin says again.

They exchange a few words. Then Dad picks me up, and jogs and then walks. Quickly. Once out of sight of Medlin he puts me down.

We walk North Terrace before taking a right on King William Road joining the masses heading to the ground. Soon we're caught up in the pace of fans striding toward the Bridge over the River Torrens near the oval's approach. It's the same bridge where I'd seen a photo of Dad and Bob as primary schoolers rugged up, hustling to the footy in coats and scarves. Hustling just like Brian was.

I don't ask Dad about Medlin and he doesn't explain. Maybe he guesses that ASIO would have a file on his old mate, and is angry that Brian has dared to flaunt their association.

I am about to turn eight. I just figure Dad doesn't want to talk to him, but I can tell he is unsettled. To complicate his feelings, Dad is secretly against the Vietnam War. He doesn't want any of his sons conscripted.

At the oval, a wet, dirty, howling rain arrives. Fans in raincoats cover their heads with newspapers. Shades of black and gold and double blue mingle. There are lines of people, almost cheek to cheek. A splash of colour and noise as we hurry through the turnstiles. The sound becomes more frenzied when the teams run out as small bits of paper blow across the ground.

Trainers in white clothing rush to position as cheer squads wrestle with their banners. The rain pelts harder after the opening siren. Umbrellas go up and I taste raindrops on my lips. My dad seems to be over the Medlin encounter. He laughs and smiles at me after another thunderclap from the skies.

We only last until half-time but Sturt wins by 28 points.

Medlin was a progressive, a professor of philosophy who despite resistance (from academia) introduced women's studies to Flinders University. He also inspired many students including John Schumann of Red Gum and the song 'I was Only 19'.

Medlin was once taken down to the River Torrens by police

and given a clear message: 'Your behaviour isn't appreciated.'

He was charged with resisting arrest and thrown in jail, where he spent three weeks. Put there by the same police force that is soon be discredited for its part in the murder of visiting gay English law lecturer George Duncan.

A dramatic photo appeared on the front page of *The Advertiser*. Medlin splaying his arms wide caught between two police. Then another in *The News* with his hair and beard shaved.

Years later Dad mentions the bawdy letters Brian wrote to him from the Victoria River Downs station, where he transported cattle to the rugged and diverse coast of Western Australia.

Dad wished he'd kept those letters. Almost fifty years after they went to school together they met for the final time at an Adelaide Tech reunion. They didn't talk much.

December 1973. Mum is training to go back to work as a nurse. She's doing another refresher course although she never looks refreshed to me. She's always busy cleaning, dusting, vacuuming or making our meals. Mum drives a small green Mini Minor and waves her fingers through the top of the car window when she passes me riding to school.

'Yoo-hoo,' she yells as she slows down and beeps.

My eldest brother Steve is nineteen, John eighteen, Ralph fifteen. I've just turned ten. Mum's taking the first steps out of her marriage. She threatened to leave when I was one, return to nursing and live in the Royal Adelaide Hospital. Dad would have lost the rental subsidy for our government housing. Back then, Dad spoke of adopting my brothers out and Mum stayed. Even if she was only half-serious about leaving, in their own way they were both trapped. Then came England and happier times. But now here we are with a growing animosity.

While Mum works as a nurse, she is temporarily freed from the constant pressures of raising young children. It is strange at first to see her getting dressed in her uniform and heading out the door. She goes shopping in the city, dressed 'to the nines' in tight black pants with her hair up in a bun. Some days she wears a red coat she bought in England that makes her look a bit like Princess Margaret, the royal who always seems to be in trouble.

Mum arrives home, full of laughter, telling her friend Flora on the phone how she was propositioned walking along Rundle Street.

'How about it?' he asked.

'I told him I had a husband and four kids, and you should have seen him take off. I haven't laughed so much for ages.'

It seems strange, somebody asking your mum out.

She's spoken to me about creepy blokes before.

In her twenties she was followed by an older man wearing a coat and fedora hat as she walked to the Palais Royal dance hall to meet Dad. The creep was there behind her on the way from the nursing quarters at the Royal Adelaide Hospital. He was even there when she ducked into a shop and hid for a while. Then Dad arrived early, halfway between the nurses quarters and the dance hall. The man following her vanished into the night as silently as he had appeared.

The sunlight winks through the clouds on the day Mr King, a kind-hearted year four teacher asks my friend Anthony to walk outside. Anthony's dad has just died of a massive heart attack.

He owned a Mobil service station on the corner of Hay Road near our school. You'd find it still if you walked to where Sunnyside Road snaked its way around Beaumont, where Sunnyside and Hay roads collide.

Some Fridays Anthony and I walked home together.

He'd duck in to see his dad and emerge with a handful of lollies.

'Here, have some of these.'

There'd be Fags, Wagon Wheels, Wizz Fizz, raspberries and chocolate frogs. Anthony's dad in oil-covered overalls made sure the lollies were shared.

'They're not all for you Anthony,' he'd say.

After the walk with Mr King, Anthony is away from school for a few weeks.

Then Mum tells me what happened. The service station is sold. Anthony's mother drops him off and picks him up from school from then on. With things rapidly going downhill at home, his dad's death is just another thing for me to worry about.

Test debutante Jeff Thomson appears lost in the middle of the MCG. His long hair creeps out from under a cap that slightly tilts. It's not long after Christmas, 1972. The next school year is so far away it hasn't entered my mind.

I can just make out my next-door neighbour Craig's black and white TV over the back of his dad's head where he's sitting on the couch. Mr Law wears stubbies and a singlet, and has a beer in hand. It's one of those TVs with a circular knob to turn the channels. Click, click, click. If you're not careful you can go past two channels in one go.

On a baking-hard MCG pitch, Australia is playing Pakistan,

and Ian Chappell's just declared at 5 for 441. The players return to the cool of a dressing room from the heat that radiates off the concrete stands.

Dennis Lillee bowls his first over. Then it's the new boy with the new ball. The sound of bat hitting ball echoes around the ground as the camera reveals rows of the empty wooden seats.

Mr Law is solidly built and has an air of authority. An aura of respect, in a 'don't fuck with me' way.

'Hello Mr Law.'

In those days there was no talking to your friend's father like he was your best mate.

'Hello son.'

I never heard him raise his voice. Just a simple 'don't do that son' if he was annoyed.

The picture on the television is grainy, like when man walked on the moon three and a half years earlier. We had a half-holiday at school, but I played footy in the front yard in the rain instead of watching it, a fact my friends struggle to believe. However, there are no giant leaps for mankind today.

On the tele, Thomson seems flat, like there's something wrong.

'I thought this bloke was quick,' I hear Mr Law say.

'C'mon,' says Craig, urging us to move.

Kids left parents in peace and quiet back then.

Craig's a year older. He's tall and blond and streetwise. In his mouth, opinion becomes fact; at least it does in my eyes.

He's not big on cricket but can be tempted into playing the odd game, tennis ball only. He's also another sucker for an early nick outside the off stump to the wall that acts as a wicketkeeper.

Craig and I unpack the board game Squatter. It's a game about being a sheep farmer in Australia but I don't really understand how to play it.

'You run your own sheep station,' Craig tells me.

When he spreads the different plastic markers and fake money out on the board and explains the rules, it seems complicated. I struggle to see the meaning in the game when there's a Test match to watch in the next room. The afternoon meanders while Mr Law snoozes intermittently in his armchair.

I shuffle through the room and pause for a moment. Always dreaming of cricket.

Thomson was a disappointment, but this was BT. Before Thommo. Before he'd almost touch the ground with the back of his hand as he wound it back. Before he'd make the ball jump from a length in a Test match. Before he was a heart-throb.

He's injured but we don't know it, and uncertain under a baggy green cap. The camera zooms in, as much as it could in those days. He walks awkwardly to deep fine leg.

Thomson goes for more than a 100 without taking a wicket, the figures of one-Test wonders.

I run out the back door of the Laws' house, through their driveway, and jump over the mini hedge, almost landing on Snoopy as he scurries out the way.

A few days later Australia wins the Test by 92 runs.

Jeff Thomson disappears after the *Sydney Morning Herald* screams: 'Thomson hurt, out of cricket'. He has a split bone in his foot. Thomson is unable to walk for a week after the Test match.

He played injured and isn't selected again for Australia for another three years. He probably thought if he didn't play he might never get picked for Australia again.

Back then, life seems simple, but it is also full of shades of grey. But playing hurt isn't the answer.

5. Stigma and secrets · 1974

Adelaide is conservative. Mum and Dad are strict and encourage Christian values. Church attendance is expected even though my parents rarely go. My brothers showed their disdain bypassing Sunday School, taking their collection money to the local deli. My parents worried about their boys being lured into 'bad ways'. Mum turfs one of Steve's friends out of our house because she's just shacked up with her boyfriend. I hear the word 'slut', as the front door slams in the girl's face.

Progressive opinions are frowned upon in the blue-ribbon Liberal eastern suburbs of Adelaide, especially those of the South Australian Labor Premier Don Dunstan, whose flamboyant lifestyle raises eyebrows.

'Be careful up there, that's where the poofs live.'

That's what some of the kids and parents in the street say about the two gay men who lived at the top of our street. Their house is surrounded by a large brown brick wall. They knew how to hold a party. Numbers of cars stretch along the street as music rattles from tinny speakers around the neighbourhood.

If ever I ask what the noise is, I am told 'It's just the poofs at it again'.

But that's the way gay people were described, either that or as 'homosexuals', with the emphasis on *homo*.

When I take Snoopy for a stroll up Lascelles Avenue, he sniffs around the street signpost where all the dogs living nearby take a piss. I never go up there at night and I walk quickly, as I have been told to do.

I now wonder why they were so poorly treated, but I've got a fair idea. It was just another prejudice in the 1970s. People assumed all gay men were pedophiles.

We are a one-car household. Dad catches two buses to work and back each day, while Mum ferries us to school and sport. Some days I walk to school, other times I chuck my bag on my back and take my bike.

I ride like the wind down Lascelles. Then chicken out. Slow down so I don't go 'arse over tit'. That's what I've heard Steve say: 'Don't go arse over, like the time you were looking at your shadow on your bike. Or the time you put your foot in the bike spokes just to see how it felt.'

It didn't feel too good.

'What did you do that for?' Mum said to me as she bandaged up my leg. 'Any worse and I'd have to take you to hospital.' She said it with a smile in that relieved the way mothers do when they realise their child will be ok.

One day I'm walking to school and that's why I notice Dad sitting in a police car as it drives by. Just near where the laneway cuts through Devereaux Road. He waves back with a big smile like he's simply walking up Lascelles Avenue after work. At school I wonder all day why he's in a cop car.

'No, it wasn't me. You must have made a mistake,' he tells me when he gets home.

I don't push the point. I know when he wants me to stop

asking. It may be something to do with Mum getting a retired private detective to follow him on the day before our family trip to the Flinders Ranges. Dad was driving to the camping store, accidentally bypassed it and did a U-turn, to backtrack.

'Why did you do a U-turn today?' Mum asks him when he gets home.

That night they argue like never before.

'You're using my money to hire a detective to follow me?'

Mum was trying to make a case to prove infidelity. Private detectives with flashbulbs made a mint hiding in hotel room cupboards, springing husbands in bed with mistresses.

Dad wasn't having an affair. He was just trying to hire some camping gear for a family holiday. I finally get to sleep, and Dad wakes me, cradles me in his arms and takes me into their bedroom. I roll over next to Mum. Dad sleeps in my room before picking up the caravan and driving us on the 600-kilometre trip. Mum announces she's staying at home.

We're soon based at Hawker in the September sunshine. We visit Wilpena Pound and climb to the top of the rim. We explore creek beds, search for lizards and birds. One day we stop by a fence alongside grazing paddocks full of dead eagles as a warning to those that attack flocks of sheep.

We head south to Port Pirie to the smelters to watch the separation of silver, lead and zinc from ores, then make a daytrip to Iron Knob and the shipyards of Whyalla.

When we return a week later, things have calmed down a bit. It feels more like my friends' homes.

I never do discover why Dad was in the police car that day.

As their marriage fails, cricket is my escape. Posters of mainly long-haired blokes with chest hair and handlebar moustaches decorate my walls. Cricket magazines and books line spaces along my windowsill and on top of my sock drawer. If you stand on my bed, you can see our back lawn where I play cricket in the nets that Dad built, just by another bank of olive trees that decorates the backyard. If you really stretch, you can see the entire gully. It has a steep slope we slide down in the winter mud, although Mum doesn't like it when we do.

'You can clean your own clothes if you keep doing that.'

'We could slide down our driveway on a kitchen tray in England,' I complain. I can't remember it, but I've seen the slides.

'That was snow not mud.'

'It was both.'

'No is the answer. Don't you know what no means, Barry?'

Mums were good at asking that question.

Mum though is usually the Good Cop in my parents' Good Cop, Bad Cop routine. Mum is much gentler to us kids than Dad. But he softens when we go to the footy or cricket.

I go to Mum if I want a special treat, or even to plead for a more expensive Christmas or birthday present. One day she buys me some cricket gloves from Kmart after I catch her in a weak moment while she's stocking up on underwear. I play cricket as much as possible in summer and even in winter.

Some days I play with hard red composition balls, flimsy pads, pink protectors and my new gloves. I'm also the 'wanderer' of the neighbourhood, often on my blue dragster. Most days I ride past the empty block where I once found hypodermic needles and drugs in a plastic bag.

When I returned home, I'd never answered so many questions.

'Where did you find it?'

'Did you open the bag?'

'Who have you told?'

'Was anyone else around?'

'What was nearby?'

I didn't want to tell them about the dirty magazine I also found that made me linger. I'd wondered why a plastic bag caused so much fuss.

My regular haunt is the nets at Linden Park number two, with Paul and Mark, school friends who live nearby. We throw the ball down to each other. We skol from a small circular foam drink container Paul's mum has prepared. It rattles with ice when you lift it. It's so cold that when you drink too quickly, you get brain freeze. Then all I can do is go down on my haunches and hold my head, until the freeze warms.

I'm always on the move, searching for something. I'm just not certain what it is.

A shudder goes through our neighbourhood.

The teenage boy next door drove his car into a tree on a summer's night. A single-car accident on a lonely stretch of road. The police draw conclusions.

A few weeks before the crash, he'd peppered our backyard with bullets when Snoopy barked on Christmas Eve. Sprayed the doghouse, Dad's beloved little Heron sailing boat and the next-door neighbour's windows. My dad and the neighbour, Max Law, reported the incident to the police, though only after the boy's father refused to sell the gun.

When Maria down the road finds out the teenager is dead, she wants someone to blame. She chooses my dad, who is taciturn and private, not Max, who is an army veteran, largely immune to local criticism and gossip. Dad's reserved nature make him suspicious in Maria's eyes. As 'overseer' of the street's morals, she takes it upon herself to judge.

On the day of the teenager's funeral, Maria rings to speak to my father.

'I just wanted to let you know what a shame it is that boy died.'

Dad doesn't say much. He just stands in the hallway where the phone is kept by the stairs. I can tell he is hurt by the implication that by speaking to the police he has somehow played a role in the teenager's death.

Within weeks the family next door sells up and moves down south.

A work transfer is also arranged for Max, and the Law family is moved back to Sydney within months. We are the only household left standing after the fallout, but not for long.

We kids are told the teenager died suddenly of leukemia, which seems strange, even to me as a twelve-year-old.

Maria's actions are typical of the bullying gossip that some domiciled women used to assert their influence and occupy their time. It is also an indicator of their power. While the men are largely at paid work, the women run the households with a ruthless efficiency.

The 'street telegraph' is highly active. God help anyone who is on the receiving end.

My eldest brother Steve rides a motorbike and hangs out with girls who wear see-through dresses and listen to Deep Purple and Led Zeppelin. He seems cool in that 1970s way with sideburns, plays the drums in a band and uses phrases like 'it's time for us to split' when Mum calls us to go inside.

Underneath, Steve is a mass of anxiety. It shows early. Steve gets into trouble without meaning to. He arrives in class at Unley High School and clumsily dumps his bag on the classroom floor, making a lot of noise as he does. Trouble follows Steve around.

'Get out, Nicholls,' the teacher yells.

One night Steve is on his way to the Festival Theatre with a friend and his parents. Rain drizzles then thickens. The L-plate driver ferrying them all to the concert makes a misjudgement at a busy intersection and smashes into another car.

Mum and Dad are watching television, thinking their eldest son is having a great night out watching The Seekers.

Then comes the phone call from the hospital.

Steve is hospitalised for a week with lacerations and concussion.

He repeats year twelve, losing contact with his social group.

Another piece of the jigsaw is taken away.

There's a purity to the air. Premier Don Dunstan is standing on the balcony of the Pier Hotel at Glenelg.

It's January 19, 1976.

The sun reflects off the ocean under a clear blue sky. It's the sort of morning where if you won the toss, you'd bat all day. The premier is resplendent in his safari suit as a crowd of more than a thousand gathers below.

Dunstan is proving South Australia is safe from an earthquake and tidal wave. John Nash, a house painter and amateur clairvoyant from Melbourne, has predicted it. It is all part of South Australia's 'punishment' from God for leading the way in gay law reform. Some South Australians are genuinely worried, but Dunstan uses it for political theatre.

'Nothing happened. But I heard there was a helicopter flying above him,' Mum tells me the next day.

Dunstan is a paradox. He is the number-one ticketholder for the Norwood Football Club when the game is uber-macho. One day he proudly wears pink shorts into State Parliament and poses on the steps for the photographers after riding his bike to work.

Dunstan is a smart politician who broke the twenty-seven-year stranglehold on power by the Liberal and Country Party just before we returned from England in the late 1960s. He has two stints as premier: June 1967 to April 1968, and then again between June 1970 and February 1979. He fights battles on many fronts including his own largely homophobic police force in South Australia who think Don a little strange.

Under Dunstan's tenure, the Festival Theatre emerges in parts as if springing to life from the banks of the River Torrens. A moribund film industry is reinvigorated. Outdoor dining is added to the cultural fabric. There is an end to the six o'clock swill. Sleepy old Adelaide is slowly being awakened by Dunstan's progressive politics.

6. Breaking the cycle · 1975–76

The Linden Park A's are playing in the middle of the wind-swept Victoria Park Racecourse. It's the only time I ever faced a girl in school cricket. Or anywhere, apart from games of continuous cricket at school – the game where everyone gets to bowl underarm and the batsman runs around a rubbish bin. I didn't even know they played interschool cricket.

My Dunlop Volley sandshoe makes a scraping sound as I draw an imaginary line to mark centre. Excitable primary schoolers' voices drift across the oval. The blonde fast bowler's pigtails bob up and down as she runs in to bowl. I'm ruminating about my back lift.

'Short and straight, short and straight, short and straight.'

The stumps are loose in the sand and sway back and forth in the strong breeze. I tap my bat gently on the ground, not quite in rhythm with the bowler's stride. She runs in, jumps, and releases the ball. I jam the bat down on the compo ball that is squeezed to fine leg. The sense of relief breaking your duck to a primary schooler is like that of saving the life of a much-loved family dog. I'm watching from the non-striker's end.

Three batsmen in a row have their stumps spread-eagled like matchsticks.

Away they shuffle to the boundary line, like water swirling

down a sinkhole. The fielders' piercing shouts and appeals are lost in the wind as each batsman departs. One by one with sunken shoulders and a look of defeat, they return.

Parents on the sidelines in deckchairs lift their heads from reading the weekend newspaper. Their chatter stills. With each dismissal, my team is more frantic as players search the untidy kit for pads, gloves, and protectors. We only have two protectors so there's this slow and embarrassing handing over of the box as the batsmen cross. The dad umpiring at square leg jogs to the stumps to borrow the incoming batsman's bat to help knock the stumps back in.

My American friend Paul walks in. No taking guard is required. Dad describes his technique as 'agricultural', but miraculously Paul connects bat to ball. There are calls of 'Yes', 'No' and 'Wait', and we scamper through for a single.

'Now you've got them on the ropes,' one of the parents calls out.

The next over we score more singles. The pressure eases. Then Paul hits a boundary with one of those straight-armed slogs that he top-edges and loops beyond the mid-wicket fielder. Now it's the fielders whose shoulders slump. Our total builds. We are back in the game. The pigtailed bowling wonder is rested. We have broken the cycle.

We walk the streets to Unley Oval. Footpaths fill, and fans wander onto the road as they edge closer to the ground.

Sturt is playing Port under bright chilly July skies. This top-of-the-table clash is big news in South Australia where the SANFL fills vistas of newspaper space and dominates talk at smoko and in schoolyards.

Today it's cold enough to make me want to wear a jumper

and hanker for a pie and hot chips. The place is packed. Close to twenty thousand are jammed into the small ground. When I go to the men's urinal, it stinks more than usual. There's always a queue and it's hard to squeeze in line to take a piss.

I finally get there and freeze. Nothing's coming out. More people appear behind me and if I could, I would look up at the roof and whistle like I've seen other blokes do.

Dad waits for me outside, ready to take me back up the slope and into the crowd. We watch the footy from the steps, shoulder to shoulder with strangers. Radios sound like a thousand wasps launching as commentators speculate on the final line-ups. The players kick end to end. There is the deep thud of boot connecting with ball as they send a screw punt distances that primary school kids can only dream about.

Ten or so cheer squad members jump the fence onto the ground. I envy them with their long hair and duffel coats, organising Sturt's banner for the players to run through. The ball is bounced, and a wall of noise strikes. The sound glides along the members pavilion out onto the oval and along the western wing where we stand.

I'm soon complaining about the umpiring and Dad repeats his mantra, 'If you don't have an umpire, you don't have a game.'

Sturt does no wrong. It's as if a higher force has intervened. Port Adelaide are helpless, like a spell has been cast on them.

By three-quarter time, Sturt is up by six goals, and my favourite player Paul Bagshaw has seven off his own boot. All is well in the world. I ask Dad if I can go and listen to Sturt's coach Jack Oatey speak.

'Yes, but make sure you check carefully where we are: look at the advert on the boundary and then the scoreboard to get your bearings, so you know how to get back to me.'

He's trying to help orientate me just like he does when he stands behind the goalposts at school footy providing a smaller target with two fingers stuck out like a goal umpire when I kick for goal.

Dad holds my footy *Budget* and I run out and forget everything he said. I'm soon among the milling crowd wanting to get close to our heroes. I pause, turn around, and all I see is a sea of faces.

'She'll be right. I'll just run in a straight line back to where I was.'

The excitement of being near the Sturt players removes any fear of what might happen next.

Oatey, all five feet four, is in the middle of the players sitting on the canvas. He's old-fashioned, wears a tie and blue jumper and addresses his men calmly. Trainers hustle around giving the exhausted team water. Oatey hobbles, shifting his weight from foot to foot, urging his charges for one last effort to put Port away.

'One more quarter is all I want but this game is not over yet.'

Some players stare vacantly, others have their eyes closed. Their sweat-soaked backs darken the light-blue lace-up guernseys. There is the sound of trainers working on players' calves and leg muscles ... *thwack thwack thwack* ...

A siren sounds to indicate that the crowd must leave the ground. It disperses like an ocean going back out to sea. I turn and run to the edge to where I think Dad is, and look for his face in the crowd.

The late afternoon sun is in my eyes. I sprint for a bit, then stop to try to gauge where I am. As I get close to the boundary, I know I am in strife. I look at the scoreboard to try to get my bearings. My heart pounds. I get over the fence just as the second siren sounds, but still I have no idea where I am. The crowd sways and cheers as the match resumes. Tears stream down my face. Back and forth, back and forth, I walk along the back of the outer then finally sit, defeated, where the ice-cream vendors hawk their wares.

A young woman turns around. 'What happened?' she asks as she kneels.

I mumble and ramble my way through the whole story the way kids do when they're upset.

'It's ok, we'll take you to the front office.'

She buys me an ice-cream. While I lick it, I hear the loud speaker: 'Could Mr Nicholls come to the Sturt front office ... Mr Nicholls we have your lost son, Barry.' I hear the call and think, why the hell did they have to include that bit? Now everyone will know.

I've only been there a few minutes and Dad arrives. I still remember the flood of relief when I see Dad's smiling face when he turns up. He doesn't say it, but I can see him thinking that I should have listened better to his instructions.

Dad thanks the girl who helped, and we watch the final stages of the match. The siren sounds. I don't feel the joy I normally associate with a Sturt win against Port. I feel stupid. But the feeling of my heart beating so loudly like it's going to bounce through my chest has stopped.

I am reunited with Dad but the sense of being hopelessly lost stays with me forever. Lost with no landmarks to guide me back.

7. A time to act • 2014/1976

A surfer adrift a large wave as it begins to break. Clear flat white sands and a huge blue sea. I'm sitting in the surgery with Dr Best, glancing at the print on his wall. He's been my GP since Ann, the kids and I moved to Busselton five years ago and I feel like know him. We're soon talking footy. He's a Fremantle fan and they're looking good for this season. He's in good nick from paddleboarding around the Geographe Bay, about my age, but looks fit enough to be playing on the halfback flank for the Dockers.

I can relate to Dr Best. He loves sport and we can have a laugh. He has the same memories of watching the Australian cricket team as I have. Remembers when Curtly Ambrose broke Geoff Lawson's jaw at the WACA in 1988.

He had just arrived at the ground after a day working as a resident at the Fremantle Hospital.

In the lengthening shadows, a quick short ball rose suddenly. The helmeted Lawson reeled back and then fell to his knees, clutching his jaw. It looked painful even from where I was sitting, on Dad's lounge in Adelaide where it was starting to get dark.

'Ok, about these results,' Dr Best says.

I'm leaning forward.

'You do know that it's a false positive?' he says. 'There's nothing to worry about.'

'I've been researching on the internet,' I tell him, 'and I still have some questions.'

He gives me a slightly quizzical look.

'Ok, leave it with me. I'll contact the specialist. But be careful of googling too much. You can find any answer you want in cyberspace.' He can see I am worked up. 'If you need something in the meantime to take the edge off things, take some of these.'

He gives me a script for a benzodiazepine.

'But don't become reliant on them. They're strong. Use them sparingly.'

I take the script and walk out with a sense of relief but by the time I've made it home, I feel anxious again. I am starting to feel like a loser. Not that I like that term. That is the anxiety and depression speaking. It diminishes you as a person. Makes you feel less worthy. Like you don't belong or deserve to be where you are, while everyone else does. Some days I feel like I don't deserve to be on this earth. Some days it feels like I'm walking in front of an X-ray machine, where people can see right through me.

Sheets of rain and hail spread across the oval. The cold wind blows through me. Parents retreat under cover. I watch my eight-year-old son Ambrose moving about the footy field picking up kicks and having fun the way kids do with little regard for what the coach says about playing positions. There's freedom in his movement, and pleasure. The siren sounds, then he joins in the team huddle. Arm in arm with his team mates, he walks jauntily from the field toward me with a smile that beams.

I experience joy for a moment before I am carpet-bombed by my ruminations. That's how it is with acute anxiety. The blessings are small and all too brief. A crack of thunder rolls across the ground as kids scream and run for cover. Everyone around me goes about their business. I stand in the rain for a moment. Trying to feel. Something.

Three o'clock, four o'clock, five o'clock ... the hours slowly count down. It's another inexorable march toward dawn. Like the stage set of a play being slowly revealed as the curtains draw back. There are gradual signs of the new day as an increasing rumble of traffic from the nearby freeway gathers pace. Neighbours head to the gym or an early morning shift as daylight sneaks under the bedroom blinds. But nothing feels right.

It reminds me of John Lennon's song 'Crippled Inside', the jaunty lyric with dark undertones. It's from the album *Imagine*, where Lennon's head in circular glasses and sideburns floats against a backdrop of clouds. The vinyl sat in a metal-ringed holder on top of the wooden stereo Mum and Dad bought in England. Looking at it gives me comfort when our family sits down for the evening meal. I stare and hope the arguing between Mum and Dad will end.

Mum moves between the kitchen and dinner table, delivering the meal to each of us.

Attack, defend, counterattack, defend.

I learn to eat fast. So do my brothers. The faster we eat, the quicker the escape to get away from the table and the noise.

Eventually Mum goes outside for a cigarette and Dad to the lounge to watch TV. The quiet is like after a storm blows through. The damage though is largely unseen.

On bad nights when it continues beyond teatime, my brothers and I gather at the bottom of our backyard gully. We huddle as a quartet. Being the youngest, I mostly sit and listen.

'What are they arguing about this time?'

'Who knows.'

A guilty, panicked laughter echoes in our small circle of protection. We climb the gully and retreat somewhere quietly in the house. But it will start up again later in the night or first thing in the morning. I still can't remember what they were arguing about, just that it felt like a battle of wills.

We're all listening to a soundtrack to a broken marriage and pretend nothing is happening. We never mention it to anyone outside our house. But then we probably don't have to.

Psychological cracks emerge. Steve almost loses a hand in a work accident, John dials his vintage antique phone in the middle of the night, even though it is not plugged in to any line. The echo of him lifting the receiver and dialling eerily seeps through the house. One night he mistakenly pisses down the wooden stairs next to the upstairs toilet.

I'm so anxious I can't sit still.

Dad calls it a state of 'perpetual motion' but I don't understand what it means. The night after Dad and I watch Sturt win the 1974 flag at a windswept Football Park in a crowd of close to sixty thousand, I sleepwalk and shiver in the upstairs bath at midnight.

Steve finds me splashing around.

'What are you doing?'

I tell him, 'Bathing in champagne, but it's cold in here.'
In those days, mothers leant over neighbours' fences or shared quiet conversations at the greengrocers. There is no need for social media: word of a family in trouble spreads like wildfire.

Some nights I sit in the lounge watching television. Trying to come to terms with what I'd just heard. I want to go back to a better time. To the day Mum and Dad hugged standing next to the washing machine, and when I clapped them, and they simply shrugged with embarrassment.

Mum arranged marriage counselling but Dad wanted her to name specific issues. He was being the dutiful husband, bringing in a good income, taking his kids to sport, maintaining the garden as well as doing other odd jobs.

What was the problem?

The blistering nightly conflict seemed to pass him by. Or perhaps he couldn't face the 'failure' of divorce or the effect it might have on his kids.

It would have taken a miracle worker to save the marriage.

The counselling never happened.

Catch the eye. Catch the eye and go to the next link. Like a ball rolling down a hill. It's hard to stop ... impossible to look away. Information is everywhere. Even on my phone. I can't look away. Like one of those 'rubberneckers' after a car accident.

The internet is my comfort and my torture. I need to find out about the false positive and what it could mean. I wonder what the test has picked up. If not this condition, then something else.

Google ... scroll through websites, there's always something to catch my eye. The obsessive searching continues so I become sensitised to any thought of even possibly having this neurological condition. Hours and hours of energy and time wasted, trying to find answers. I long for the era before the internet, when you went to see the doctor and they explained the situation and out you went.

My anxiety is free-floating. It will launch anywhere. And land anywhere. It narrows my thinking and plays into my increasing doubts. What did I read about this last night? It's like walking down a hallway that thins with each step.

I know this isn't right. I should be as happy as can be. I have four healthy beautiful kids, but pleasure remains elusive. My addiction to looking up information can't be sated.

'Just walk away,' says Dr Best. 'No matter how compelled you feel to go back and look up more information. Just walk away. Even if it means going for a walk around the block.'

It's a sentiment that my partner Ann echoes and she grows increasingly frustrated by my anxieties. I agree with her, but when I try walking away, I get halfway down the hall and think 'There's just one more thing I'd like to check'.

I am beginning to doubt everything, which in turn makes me feel vulnerable. Then I felt guilty for feeling vulnerable. But I keep going back to look up more information. Just one last time.

Doubt and guilt have captured me, and I don't have the mental strength to ward them off.

Froth from waves crashes into rocks, floats then disappears. Wisps of cloud carry across a sky. The weather is a gift, a break from the steady stream of rain of the last month. It's more like a bright England summer's day than a Western Australian winter. Daydreaming, I imagine I'm at an oval bordering a beach at Exeter in England's south. It's June 1984 but not the Orwellian type. There's no internet or *Big Brother* reality TV, just a healthy supply of tabloid and broadsheet newspapers, vinyl, Walkmans filled with tapes, and FM radio stations to keep us all entertained.

The trip to Devon is an annual ritual for the Ashford Cricket Club, located in Middlesex but we play in the Surrey Championship League, which has an above average standard of cricketers. And there is also some fun to be had.

The tour which is spoken about for months leading into June involves a week of cricket, beers and curries. Married blokes are let free from their families for five whole days with younger men who have no responsibilities beyond work and drinking lager.

After a cold May, summer has broken. Uncoiled like a cat on a rug.

I'm sitting on a chair on the balcony of a thatch-roofed pavilion. I can feel the ocean breeze from the English Channel on my face. Deckchairs spread out where older people sit enjoying the sun's rays. It's been a day running around in the outfield. 'C'mon Bazza, chase it all the way,' a team mate calls.

A ball rolls into the picket fence.

I take in the scenery of the ocean with its sand and seashell-covered beach next to where we are playing. How lucky am I? I'm watching the bowler run in as my phone rings.

It's August 2014 and Ann's daily phone calls have a greater sense of urgency.

'Much the same,' I tell her.

It must be hard for her to hear me say it again and again, almost as difficult as it is for me to be broken from my dream.

I wait in the car to let my mind settle. Take a deep breath and open the car door. I've been at the doctor's too much lately. Normally I go no more than once a year. It's a point of pride. But now I'm as uptight as an army sentinel at a post listening for footsteps. I'm early to the appointment. That's another thing anxiety does, makes you very punctual. My next-door neighbour is a nurse at the surgery, but that's life in a country town.

'Hello,' I say and put on a smile. I'm getting good at faking things. I've had plenty of practice over the years. I wonder what she's thinking. I've been here so much. There doesn't seem to be anything obviously wrong with me.

I flick through a magazine then remember an article I read about doctors' surgeries and germs. I rub my hands together to rub the germs away. I'm checking Twitter, scrolling down. *Tap, tap, tap.* It's an enticing mix of news, gossip, and outrage but it feels like my mind is running down a hill ahead of me.

Other patients arrive and check in: older people and mothers with sick kids.

Dr Best appears and calls my name. He has the look of someone who has spent the morning in the surf.

Once when my appointment was delayed I suggested that's where he'd been.

'More like the surgery at the hospital,' he said.

I didn't make the quip again.

'You know the entire WA health system says that you don't have this condition. It is a false positive.'

Dr Best is smiling and stresses the last two words but not in an arsehole type of way. He's emphasising the point to reassure. I know what he says is true, but logic isn't at the forefront of my mind. The diagnosis is complicated, and my circular thinking heightens the sensitivity and confuses me. A misplaced comment from a nurse, and a visit to a specialist with no bedside manner and limited communication skills have already made things worse. She was more interested in ushering me out the door during the $400 appointment than providing evidence for her explanations.

There is a pause.

'Ok, how are you travelling?' Dr Best is looking me square in the eye. Like there's no escape and no changing topics this time. By now he's worked out that anxiety is the root cause of my concerns. But I'm still asking about the medical false positive. He reassures me again.

'False positives happen all the time. They are just part of the testing procedures. The tests you've had to rule out this condition are very accurate.'

'What about the false positives, what do they indicate?'

Dr Best leans forward peering over his glasses at his computer and reels some off. None of them are life-threatening but I've built even these conditions up in my mind.

'One here says a false positive can occur when you are getting older. And we can safely say that you are.' He smiles, then changes tack. 'How are you coping with the drive from Busselton to Bunbury every day?'

'I'm getting a bit sick of it to be honest.'

'What about the pressures of work?'

He knows I help produce and present a daily three-hour current affairs ABC radio program across regional Western Australia. It is a demanding job, but I love the thrill of live radio and the interactions with listeners.

'I actually feel better at work. I've never had any problem coping with the pressures. I find it stimulating.'

At this stage I am just a more intense version of what I have been at work for years. I can listen keenly, home in on any inconsistencies. Sense when politicians dodge questions more acutely than ever. I am more anxious, but at this point it helps not hinders my performance.

At times I've felt the same way playing cricket. Just nervous enough to do well but not overwhelmed.

I am also writing a book about Australia's Test side during World Series Cricket. Each night after work I line up one- to two-hour interviews. I've begun transcribing the interviews and writing. Trying to avoid worries by working at every moment I'm not sleeping, eating or trying to get back to sleep in the middle of the night.

But Dr Best knows something isn't right.

'Ok, I reckon we need a mental health plan for you.'

'What does that mean?'

'I think we need to deal with your anxiety.' He explains to me that mental health plans are funded in regional Australia, so that once your GP makes one with you, it helps you (in theory) more easily get access to services.

And that is how it all starts to play out.

8. Steve's spiral and other upheavals • 1975

Dawn breaks and I hear urgent voices. Like arrows to a target. Steve's taken an overdose of sleeping pills. It's the morning of his second-year physio exams. The shower is running as I stumble outside my bedroom past the staircase next to the toilet.

'It's no good, Les, you have to call an ambulance,' Mum yells. 'Call a bloody ambulance. Now.'

I don't know why, but Dad is holding Steve upright in the shower. My brother must somehow think he can still do his exam. Maybe Dad hopes so too.

It's a far cry from the night before when Steve gave me a quick smile and thumbs-up as he pointed to his copy of *Gray's Anatomy*. He liked to show me the intricate diagrams of the muscles and bones in the book.

'Cross your legs,' he said, making the move as he spoke. He pointed to my knee. 'The sartorius is called the tailor's muscle, because it becomes larger when you sit with a cross-legged stance, like tailors used to do at work.'

We're a world away from tailors and smiles this morning. I pace in small circles like one of the caged tigers I saw at the Adelaide Zoo when we went there for my tenth birthday.

I feel invisible. As the ambulance arrives I can't bring myself to watch even though I am worried I'll never see my brother again.

Everyone disappears. Nothing is said or explained.

Mum travels in the ambulance with Steve, and Dad drives to the Royal Adelaide Hospital.

My ride down Lascelles Avenue is slower than normal. I'm shaking but glad at least to be out of the house and feel the breeze in my face. Soon the dragster bike wheels slide into the rack behind the open-plan classroom.

I unpack my bag, clearing lost pencils and scraps of paper and make my way to my desk, hoping no one will come near or say anything. Douglas who lives a few houses up from us on Lascelles Avenue senses my distress and approaches.

'Just ignore me, please just ignore me,' I whisper to myself. My bottom lip trembles the way it does before I'm about to cry. I hold my breath and hope the feeling goes away.

'What was happening at your house this morning?'

'It's nothing,' I mumble as I continue to lay my books out on the desk.

One book slips and falls to the floor. Douglas raises his voice and leans down to speak, the way kids do when they are trying to get their own way.

'Hey Barry, why was there an ambulance outside of your house this morning?'

I'm trying to hold back the tears. And then again, he's at me.

'Hey Barry, I saw an ambulance outside your house. What happened?'

I crack into a wall of tears. Mr Norley, a tall lean teacher with black Brylcreemed hair, intervenes. He hugs me and leads me away. I'm soon sitting in the sick room waiting.

'Your dad is on his way,' says the receptionist in a gentle tone.

Dad puts on a good front as if nothing has happened.

'Steve's ok. You didn't tell anyone what happened did you?' he says as we walk together to the school gate.

It seemed an unusual question to ask at the time but now I can see why. Dad didn't want anyone judging his eldest son.

After checking I'm ok too, Dad leaves again.

I spend the day at school relieved yet drained.

That's the way it was back then: keep your dirty laundry indoors.

Steve dropped out of all his university exams. That was no secret. He was never the same again.

Douglas is also dead to me, the little cunt.

Pembroke's headmaster John Moody stares across his desk. We're out of the bright sunshine into the dim light of his office. Here for an interview for a sporting scholarship.

Moody's a former Norwood league footballer, tall, lean and grey-haired, dressed in a suit and tie, and sitting behind a large wooden desk.

I don't say much.

Dad points out that I've just been selected in the junior state cricket side. Mr Moody just nods and smiles. Like he's heard it all before, a parent trying to sell their kid to the school.

Afterwards we walk to a small parking station next to the bursar's office. Dad asks me what I think.

I shrug my shoulders. 'Different to Linden Park.'

A bell rings and a swarm of students and teachers walk between lessons.

A few months later, word comes through. I'm in.

Our Father, who art in heaven ...

I never meet her, but Sister Janet Mead is my saviour. Or at least hearing her song on a 45 single makes me feel better. The bespectacled, brown-haired nun with the clear gaze and top of the chart pop song is a contrast to the usual long-haired rock stars we listen to.

Just hearing the start of the pop version of 'The Lord's Prayer' quells the anxiety. For a while I play it every night before bed. If I play it three times and recite at least two verses clean without mistake, everything will be ok. My parents must think it is the quirk of a young mind.

I figure it is what everyone does. To stay safe. That's one of the main problems of anxiety. The feeling of fear. On edge, waiting for a catastrophe.

It is different to the nerves I feel when I play cricket.

'That's just butterflies,' Mum says as I head off to the ground.

When I am anxious I can sleepwalk with the best of them. I could have sleepwalked for Australia. One cricket trip to Queensland I am billeted with a family called the Gallaghers, along with another boy from New South Wales called David Knox, who later plays rugby for Australia. Tropical thunderstorms hammer their tin roof. It rains like it is never going to stop. Not like Adelaide rain.

I bring out the routine again. Say a little prayer. In between points when David and I play table tennis in the Gallagher's covered backyard, I stop and close my eyes and slip in a quick prayer.

'What are you doing?'

'Just pausing.'

'Ok, play.'

Then I serve the next ball.

David and I are shopping in the Brisbane CBD. We walk around a sports store looking at cricket bats and tennis balls.

David sidles up to me.

'Did you steal something?'

'No.'

'See that woman over there? She's been following you around the store.'

I am stopped and asked to empty my pockets. All the security guard finds is crumpled paper from a lunchtime treat.

When Mr Gallagher hears about it he rings the store to complain.

'This boy is from South Australia representing his state, what sort of impression do you want to give him of Queensland?'

The next day a new pair of junior-sized batting gloves is delivered to my billet family's house.

'Here you go, a little memento,' says Mr Gallagher.

I'd never heard that word before.

One night I sleepwalk out into the middle of the storm, before making it into my hosts' bedroom, discarding my pyjama pants as I go. Mrs Gallagher drowsily dries me and helps me back to my own bed. Another morning I find myself lying at the base of David's bed like a cat curled up in a ball.

'Hey, mate, what are you doing?'

Our billets take David and me to the Gabba to watch a one-day match between Queensland and South Australia. I'd watched from afar the First Test against the West Indies. Now I marvel at the Gabba's dog track, just outside the oval, and the way the noise echoes around the ground. Jeff Thomson ambling to the crease. The ball jumping up from a good length. South Australian batsmen dance around the crease, looking anxious. But not half as anxious as I feel.

Going to the new school feels like I'm running late to catch a bus.

Some students already know each other, and cliques between the others soon form. Classmates wear slightly ripped jeans and Puma or Adidas tops for the once-a-term casual day for a silver coin donation. My plain baggy jeans curl at the bottom; Mum hasn't had the chance to turn them up properly. They drag under my Dunlop Volley sandshoes, beginning to fray.

I am close to thirteen but I'm longing for the golden days of primary school like a fifty-year-old trying to bring back the glory days of their twenties.

'When are you going to score some runs, you loser?' he asks out the corner of his mouth as he passes me in the schoolyard. He knows I am there on a sporting scholarship because he is too. A much taller boy with a gift for taking high marks in footy, he hisses at me daily throughout the summer months.

He sniggers as he walks, turning his head just enough to stare at me to remind me of how much of a failure I am. By the end of first term my top score is 10. That is from a house match, where some kids who don't know one end of a cricket bat from another are forced to play to make up the numbers.

I am struggling on turf pitches, where I have to use my own strength rather than the pace of the ball bouncing off a concrete surface.

I'm not much good at schoolwork either. It feels like I am caught in a sinking pile of mud.

Science. Fail.

Maths. Fail.

Life. Fail.

Or that is how it feels.

Frank Sinatra is singing 'Strangers in the Night' on the radio. Mum sits opposite me in the lounge with a sad look on her face.

'We need to have a talk, Barry.'

I haven't seen her look like this before. There's no gentle expression.

The house is quiet, and Dad has gone out. I hope that maybe she's going to tell me that we're finally going to get a pool in the backyard. She'll act all serious and then spring it on me like a surprise. Maybe I'm getting a Puma tracksuit, to make up for the robot I missed out on a few years back after I had my tonsils out.

Mum continues talking. I watch her lips move but I'm not really registering what she is saying. I hear words coming out of her mouth but not in sync with her lips. Not as complete sentences. Then I begin to listen more closely.

'I'm leaving your father.'

I look outside. Frank Sinatra is still crooning but what I'm hearing is too painful, so I start thinking about whether I can kick the footy the length of the front lawn.

'Are you listening, Barry?'

Then I realise and absorb the gravity and start to cry. 'Do you think that you'll ever get back together?'

She starts to laugh and then stops herself. 'No, I don't think so.'

I still hold out hope that they will.

It is hard for Mum to have this conversation. No wonder Dad has gone out.

After she leaves, Mum is at pains to point out that there are different types of love. It is her way of saying she has left Dad but not us kids.

I wonder if life can get any worse. Then I get a sign it easily can.

A very serious family lives down the road. The children are friendly but the parents distant. They have a tennis court, but the environment is sedate. Visiting kids are not welcome. Especially loud ones like me.

Middle-aged men and women dressed in white play on a beautifully manicured court. There is the gentle *thwack* of ball on racquet; classical music plays in the background. It is soothing and peaceful. Our house could have done with some classical music.

Silver trays with drinks perched atop are brought onto their court to complete the occasion. The dad, Mr S, has a keen interest in violin making.

'For God's sake, stop screaming out!' he shouts over the fence. 'The whole world can hear you!'

I am playing next door at Martin's house. And commentating. A little too loudly it seems.

Mr S is always in a barely controlled hurry, rushing to work and home again, fussing over his tennis court maintenance with the utmost care, polishing his classic hardtop MGB coupe. He's about to go with his family on a year's sabbatical in Italy, on a Churchill Fellowship.

But instead he drops dead on his tennis court. At the age of fifty-three.

'Let that be a lesson to you,' says Dad to me that night. 'All that rushing around for nothing. He lost decades trying to save a few minutes.' But he says it gently.

Martin's dad is the complete opposite. He's a grey-haired, slightly balding, orthopaedic surgeon who drives a Porsche. He knows how to relax and often joins in our games in the pool. He's also interested in my cricket.

'When are you going to score a double century?' he asks.

'That might be a bit hard.'

'You can do it, Barry. Just put your mind to it and you never know what might happen.'

That's why I love going to Martin's house. Anything seems possible and no one cares if I commentate loudly.

Five days of swimming, playing tennis, a bivouac, canoe rides and sharing in the cooking and cleaning and, most importantly, hanging on not to do a shit. Eventually I sneak away to the dorm toilets. Everyone is distracted outside. I can hear sounds of kids playing tennis and four square, bouncing basketballs or calling out to each other. I figure I'm safe. Check for toilet paper, clean the seat and let loose.

It's the most at peace I've felt for a week. Then ... I hear rustling. Excited voices with a bounty of yabbies. They know they're not supposed to bring the crustaceans into the dorm but that only adds to their excitement.

I stay in the toilet but the stink seeps out.

Then slowly: 'What's that smell?'

More voices join in. 'Oh no, who did that, has something died in here?'

Girls come in from outside to hear what the fuss is about.

'Who's responsible for that?'

Laughter bounces across the dormitory. Like a horror show. 'Quick, we have to save the yabbies!'

A shuffling of sandshoes on concrete floor, the sound of kids quickly gathering up fishing nets and rods. I think it's ended. Then the bully appears as I'm still sitting on the toilet. As I try to lift my feet off the floor, he appears with cloth around his neck like Lawrence of Arabia standing on the seat in the next cubicle.

'It's Nicholls, quick, escape.'

Ten minutes later I emerge. Hoping they've all left. But they're waiting for me. The bus trip home is lonely and anxious. My hope for a better year eight after the camp has disappeared like water down the kitchen sink when it makes a loud, swirling noise.

When the final bell of that year rings, relief washes over me.

Childhood memories soon disappear to dust.

Mum and Dad separate. I'm the only one in my year who comes from a broken home. That's the way it's described.

New no-fault divorce laws only require evidence of twelve months separation. My parents are among the first in the country to use them when they divorce in 1978.

Dad moves to the next suburb in a tin-roofed three-bedroom house with a greenhouse out the back and a balcony overlooking the city. Mum shifts to a two-bedroom unit in Beulah Park, a walkable distance to school. She avoids pressing Dad for maintenance payments and I spend half a week at each house. Ralph shares his time between Dad's and his girlfriend Meredith's flat. John has moved to Laverton in remote Western Australia where he works for a mining company, while Steve and his seventeen-year-old girlfriend Bronwyn live in an eastern suburbs unit.

My two eldest brothers, fed up with the arguing at home, have become only occasional visitors. By the time Mum leaves, our family dynamic has become like a dam that has almost reached bursting point, and the consequences of managing all that tension will be felt by each of us in different ways decades down the track.

In the aftermath though, there are glimmers of relief and light. It is Mum who introduces me to Rudyard Kipling's 'If' and Max Erhmann's 'Desiderata', which she sticks to the fridge door. And she spends hours knitting a woollen cricket jumper for me with the green and gold colours, adding a cable design for authenticity, like the ones the Australian cricketers wear.

I meet my mum's new boyfriend on New Year's Day 1977, the first day of the Second Test of the summer against Pakistan at the MCG. A small white fox terrier jumps up and down, yapping, as Larry pulls his ute into the small car park next to us.

I feel a mixture of jealousy and relief. When Larry is around, Mum is calmer, at least in the early days of their relationship. The car radio hums with the cricket commentary from the MCG. Australia's opening batsman Rick McCosker is out first ball, LBW, embarrassingly padding the ball away from the gentle medium-pace bowling of Asif Iqbal.

Larry bounces out of his car followed by Rex, who must be coaxed down from the seat to the concrete.

'Cosier and Greg Chappell are still in. Did you see the way McCosker got out?'

Inside the pub, a small television in the corner replays the dismissal via one-camera angles and small commentary teams. Heads at the bar crane toward the screen with each delivery.

Soon Mum's ordering a Coke for me, and two shandies for Larry and her.

I don't know what to make of Mum's new friend. They met at Alexandra Lodge, where Mum works as a nurse and he is a tradesman.

Larry occasionally rang at Lascelles in the dying days of my parent's marriage.

'Don't call here,' Dad angrily responded before hanging up the phone. 'Bloody janitor, why is he ringing here?' he'd whisper under his breath, though I could still hear him.

Larry makes Mum laugh, which I haven't seen for a while. After school he sits shirtless at Mum's dining room table drinking a longneck beer. Tufts of hair protrude from his barrel chest.

Nanna doesn't like Larry.

'A man shouldn't sit at the table with his shirt off. They should have more respect.'

Some days when Mum isn't home in time from work, Larry drops in. He greets me with a warm smile and seems to have an interest in whatever I am doing.

Mum has told me that Larry suffered shell shock from his days fighting the 'Japs' in the Second World War in Papua New Guinea. I ask him if he killed anyone.

'A couple of Japanese boys,' he answers, after a moment's hesitation.

Despite his charms, there is something dark about him. As their relationship develops, Mum has long conversations on the phone in her bedroom with him, sometimes in tears.

'Larry's drunk again.'

I don't like to see Mum like that. She once asks me what I would think if Larry moved in. I feel bad because I think she wants me to agree but I just can't.

Their relationship lasts a few more years and then Larry stops coming around. I sometimes see him driving around town with Rex sitting in the seat next to him. For some reason he always seems to be in a hurry. We later find out Larry has a girlfriend in Adelaide and a wife interstate.

I don't know if his war stories were true.

Steve announces he's marrying his teenage girlfriend. Bronwyn's dad played cricket for South Australia in the 1950s. That's the only interest I have in her. She sees me as competition for my brother's affection and dismisses anything I say.

They marry in an Unley park near where they live. The reception is austere and the mood tolerable, not the joy you'd expect at a wedding. Mum and Dad won't stand next each other in the wedding photos and Bronwyn's parents can barely contain their rage at their daughter getting married so young.

Steve commutes from Victor Harbour to Adelaide to work while Bronwyn looks after their small hobby farm. Work and the commute put undue pressure on Steve and it is the beginning of the end of their marriage

It's like Steve and Bronwyn and their relationship are out of luck from the start – a couple of kids both choosing marriage as a way to escape their unhappy home lives.

Tears flow in the days before year nine.

'I hate that school and never want to go back.'

Mum and Dad are talking quietly, almost in collaboration.

Dad takes me to the city for a day out. Down Greenhill Road, along Dequetteville Terrace, past Prince Alfred College where

I was bowled around my legs for one last summer when the coach told me it must have been a good ball.

Dad's brown Cortina eases into Rundle Street, past the Stag pub on the corner and up the winding concrete to the top floor of the new multistorey car park. In a couple of years it will be lined with metal cages to stop people throwing themselves off.

Out we hop and walk past the newly minted Malls Balls and arrive at the Balfours store. I feel a lift in my senses that I haven't felt for ages.

'Feeling peckish?'

I nod, growing in confidence with every step along Rundle Mall. The smell of pastry hits me as we enter. There's Kitchener buns with dollops of jam, sugar and cream, chocolate doughnuts, Berliners, vanilla slices, custard tarts, all laid out like an art display.

Various goodies are scooped up and paid for. We stroll beside the River Torrens. Ducks scatter when the Popeye paddleboat drifts by and blows its horn.

I want the day to last forever.

We are approached by an Englishman with a flat hat, and one of those bags around his waist, like kids who sell footy budgets at the Adelaide Oval.

'Great day for a paddle, guvnaah.'

I wonder what a 'guvnaah' is.

Dad holds my arm to make sure I get safely into the paddleboat. It's two people to a boat. Joggers scurry around the paths that line the river. We take a few minutes to get into rhythm of paddling and then we're away. Like a batsman who's just started to middle the ball.

'School will get better. It just takes time. It's a brand new year.'

Dad, who was briefly a teacher, tells me how much he enjoyed the start of the school year and the chance for a clean slate, to begin again. The excitement the first day brings, the smell of new books.

A fresh start is how he describes it.

The day passes in a rush. As afternoon shadows form, we walk back to the city.

'Don't worry, I'm sure the teachers are probably feeling a little nervous as well.'

I have the same feeling I have when I get off the mark in cricket.

9. An unsplendid isolation · 2014/1977–78

A shadow blends us as one. I'm lying on the grass at my eldest daughter Jacy's sports day, turning slightly to the right, with a half-smile. Three-year-old Ellie lies on my back, her arms wrapped tightly around my neck. She wears a pink hat and one of those forced smiles kids have when a camera hovers.

I should have been full of joy. But I was still worrying. Worrying about the 'what ifs' in life. I doubted everything. What if the confirming test that I didn't have this condition was wrong, what if they used a different test last time? What if all the misinformed crap I'd been reading on the internet was right? Intrusive thoughts bumped my logic away.

'What if?' reminds me of Dr Goria in a small room with a circular table in the middle, on one of my worst days, when I questioned everything.

'What if?' said Dr Goria. 'But what if?' He kept saying it. It's the only time he had sounded even remotely frustrated with me. 'Look at the evidence, this is the circular thinking that you are caught in.'

He's right. It feels like the wiring in my brain is caught on repeat. But for some reason I keep asking the question.

The ball rolls from grass to dirt and into the wire fence as the teacher signals four runs. The kids on the sidelines clap in support. Term one, six weeks in. Life is better. I'm scoring runs.

The 1977 Centenary Test looms. The celebration of 100 years of Test cricket that begins on a Saturday in March, seasonally late for a Test match in Australia. The ABC and Channel Ten televise the game, with Keith Miller and Frank Tyson, Richie Benaud and Geoff Boycott all giving their views.

It's a cricket feast, as morning and afternoon papers are saturated with coverage. More than 200 Australian and England ex-Test players gather at the Hilton Hotel. Bill Watt prepares a green-tinged pitch. The hype is enormous, bigger than the 1956 Olympics. Lightbulbs flash. A specially minted coin is tossed. Tony Greig sends the home side in.

Mr Davis is fighting against the tide; half the class is out the door. It's nearing the end of term one.

'Remember to write your homework down.'

I race along the balcony, down the steps onto the playground, past the four-square courts where a tall gum tree drops its leaves sparingly across the yard.

A steep pavilion dedicated to former pupils who lost their lives during the First World War overlooks Haslam Oval, an oasis of green next to the boarding house, where ivy creeps along its edges. The radio in my bag is turned on. The sound vibrates from among my schoolbooks.

Commentators sum up the action of the final day's play. They speak to the backdrop of a sound like humming bees. With each step comes a greater sense of freedom. Closer to home to watch the action on Mum's TV. I wait at the crossing on the Parade to begin the sprint. Impatience grows. Like a tap, tap, tap of your foot, when you can't contain yourself. I join the mass of movement of kids en route to athletics practice.

'C'mon, hurry up.'

Green light. Bag slips, some books scatter. They are quickly regathered and off I go. A shortcut past the pavilion and the PE teachers setting up for after-school sports. 'Down the guts' of Haslam Oval. That's what last year's footy coach says. Then a deviation, past the gum trees that ring the oval. Swing the gate next to the cricket nets. Left at Beulah Road, beyond the brick veneer homes with small flowerbed gardens and metal fences. Turn right at Osborne Avenue and rush through Mum's front door. Bag lands on couch. Snoopy the cocker spaniel, his tongue hanging out, yelps and jumps up too. I lunge for the television. Switch on and wait for it to turn from dark grey to the illumination of the MCG.

Mum planned her departure strategically with some financial help from Nanna, and made sure she would still have people around her after she left. She'd already met Larry, was back at work and bought a two-bedroom unit. Mum also arranged for Heather (a former next-door neighbour and wife of a work friend of Dad's) to come over once a week. She had other friends like Flora, Gwen and Shirley who called in frequently.

I couldn't name one friend of Dad's apart from his brother Bob and an old university mate, Harold Gilbert, who we rarely saw. Dad didn't even tell his work colleagues in his carpool that Mum had left.

Throughout year nine, things slowly change for me at school. I'm making more mates and begin to hold more than two-word conversations with girls. I even walk with a greater sense of confidence, like a batsman who really wants to get out into the middle and face the bowling.

Life improves for Dad as well as he starts to come to terms with Mum leaving and the loss of mutual friendships over their divorce. When Dad picks me up at Gary and Greg's house after eight ball on Friday nights, their parents Brian and Heather ask him in for a drink. They sit on the couch, eat some nibbles and talk.

The sense of generosity and welcoming that shines out of the room is like a ray of light. It's one of the few times Dad socialises away from work.

At our new house in Dutton Street, next-door neighbour Max Ey knocks on the door, his face partly buried by the shade of a big straw hat.

'Just thought I'd drop in to introduce myself. My wife Eileen and I have just moved in and we'd like to ask you and your son over for a meal.'

It is only a small gesture but it means the world to my dad.

It's September 2014 and I've got an anxiety I can't wash away. Not even in a warm shower on a cool morning. The thoughts keep coming. Exercise is normally the answer, the endorphins kicking in like a drug. I push hard on a stationary bike and tune out before lifting some weights. Listen to music videos and feel the sweat gathering in my hair, dripping down my face. The more I do, the better I feel.

But this time I feel like I've been dragged under by a wave. Tossed and turned. I have no control over what is happening. Nothing works: no matter how big a perspiration I've built up, the post-exercise high doesn't arrive. It's like one of those dreams where you run but can't move forward. Isolation creeps into life.

I can't name one friend I have in Busselton, and I'm losing contact with my old Adelaide mates.

I'm dodging raindrops walking toward chemistry class. Up the steep stairs to the science lab. Holding the front page of the *Advertiser*.

I spot Gary who's taking his books out of his bag and spreading them on a long lab bench. He's in the middle row. Far enough back to be lost in the crowded class. The revelations about Kerry Packer in the paper and his signing of Australia's top cricketers is like a bolt of lightning.

'Have you seen the paper?' I demand, waving it in front of Gary's face.

'Yeah, I did. I dunno what to make of it, to be honest.'

Gary is more nonchalant than I expected. Maybe the news is still sinking in. Maybe he doesn't take it all as seriously as I do. Not many do. Kerry Packer – not that we know who he is – has bought out the best of Australian cricket talent. Packer knows the administrators have treated the players shabbily regarding pay and conditions but most importantly he wants the rights to televise cricket, a cheap form of entertainment for Channel Nine and its affiliates.

We don't really know what it all means. We sense the Aussies are struggling for form on their tour of England. Hesitant batsmen nicking to the slips. There's a string of low scores. Like I feel in chemistry class where I haven't a clue. Fielders feel the chill from the arctic-like weather. They wear thick woollen jumpers and stand with folded arms in the field.

The teacher, Mr Campbell, an unassuming Scotsman in

his thirties, stands in front of the blackboard. Coloured chalk is spread on a metal railing behind him. He's busy moving between the rows of long desks, checking the Bunsen burners. Like a cricket captain sorting the field out, while students slouch on their stools.

Hormones run amok as textbooks and bags are dumped like mini explosions. Mr Campbell has the periodic table out. I like the shape of the chart and the way it's neatly arranged. I could design a decent cricket board game out of it. He rubs his hands together, which is what defines him from other teachers. He does it in the same way that Ian Chappell used to, organising the field before the first delivery is bowled.

'Ok, listen up.'

Most of the class carry on with business. Megan and her offsider Colleen shuffle in. Late again. Both with curly brown hair, blue-eyed, with bodies developed beyond their age, and confident. Mr Campbell is trying to grab the class's attention. But it's the dynamic duo attracting the eyeballs. He's unimpressed with their late arrival. But he has unrealistic expectations. He expects us to automatically remember the symbols of the periodic table. It's not something important like Don Bradman's average (99.94). The lesson passes in a blur. The siren sounds. En masse, students rise and walk to their next class. A Megan- and Colleen-inspired erection means I linger. Pack the books into my bag while sitting. No easy task. Once things have settled I make it past the cool kids gathering as they always do near the tuck shop. Some sit on a bench. Others stand. They mock passers-by. Like me from under the pergola.

'Hey Barry, how's the cricket going?'

The usual shit. But I walk on by. I am no longer alone. There are four of us now. Gary and Greg as well as Sam. We're eating snacks as we talk. It's hard to hear what each other is saying. Words spilling out in mumbled form.

The bell rings and we scatter. Like leaves in the wind.

When I get home, I read Ian Chappell's *Passing Tests* about the 1972/73 summer when Pakistan toured and the Australian team visited the West Indies. I'm sitting at my new desk with the map of the world on it. I sit there because it's quiet from Mum's complaints about Dad, even though they separated a year ago.

It's year ten, 1978, and the song on Mum's turntable lasts a lucky three minutes thirty seconds. 'Movin' Out' by Billy Joel.

I don't tell Gran when Dad and I pop in at her house at Mile End, as I know she hasn't heard of Billy Joel. It's track one from *The Stranger*, the first album I own. A fifteenth birthday present from Steve.

My oldest brother's going through a stage of buying and giving records to just about everyone he meets, especially on your birthday.

He has some money as he's working as a physiotherapist at the Home for Incurables. Me and my brothers and their partners all gather at Mum's once a week for a meal. I feel guilty when anything bad is said about Dad, who's not there. And some of what Mum says doesn't fit my version of Dad.

I discover other songs from the album, like 'Scenes from an Italian Restaurant'. Of old lovers Brenda and Eddie, meeting again.

Pity Mum and Dad aren't quite as friendly. When they meet each week to drop me off, my anxiety peaks. On special occasions we all eat at the Pagoda Chinese Restaurant not far from Dad's house, and we share food from the lazy Susan. Mum and Dad sit at opposite ends of the table. The aroma of sweet and sour pork and braised steak with cashew nuts and sizzling steak fills the room. Some nights the owner, in a red dazzling coat, plays the piano while his wife sings.

We sit on hard wooden chairs. Read textbooks on desks with round indents for the ink bottles. Carved initials of students' declared loves stare out. I wonder where Tony, who loved Annabel, is now. Mrs A, a history teacher with an Oxford accent, uses a stream of sentences that I associate with a smart person on TV. Not the type you'd see on *Countdown*. She's in her forties. I think my mum is good at talking but Mrs A has her covered. Well and truly. Generously proportioned, Mrs A wears a floral decorated dress that hangs off her like a circus tent billowing in and out with a strong breeze. Today she is particularly flustered and keeps pushing her unkempt greying hair across her brow. She adds a flourish to emphasise the stress we are causing her, as beads of sweat drip down her forehead.

Mrs A is an expert on medieval European history and relishes telling the stories of murder and mayhem. She seems to have the wisdom of Yoda from *Star Wars*. But there's only so much history a teenage schoolboy can take, especially when it's not about cricket. Tim, a bright, red-haired kid with a love for the indulgent English public schoolboy Billy Bunter, senses my distraction and shoots me a glance.

'Think of Britt,' he says with a twinkle in his eye, referring to the Swedish model Britt Ekland, aka Rod Stewart's girlfriend. The girl on the poster he keeps in his schoolbag and furtively brings out some lunchtimes to show us. Like an antique dealer with a prized painting.

'Thinking of Britt always worked for me.'

He says it in a way that a doctor might when you leave their surgery, taking a script with you.

When Mrs A speaks, she pauses. A lot.

She's got the art of the pause even more refined than Richie Benaud when he commentates.

Each time she does, the class, almost as one, looks up. I wonder if she's heard Tim. But today she has an expression of resignation.

Anger has ceded to defeat. She takes a breath and looks sullen. 'One day,' she says, 'I can promise you that life will lay you out flat, no matter what you do. Your life will come crashing down. One day you'll think back to this moment and believe that this ancient woman who taught you history was right.'

When she stops, Mrs A stares above our heads toward the back of the room. A murmur of unease rumbles around the class. Glances and smiles are exchanged between kids who have had little time for each other. For once as a class we are united. In our joy. Our teacher has 'lost it'. The siren sounds, and we stumble out of the room. Like ants tumbling from a water-filled hole.

Thirty-eight years later, I finally understand what she was saying.

I shout at the sky: 'Now I hear you, Mrs A.'

'Sign the book guys,' says a young woman with a tight-fitting Puma tracksuit and a big smile.

Why do I need Britt Ekland for a distraction when I can just go to the PE shed? She is another in a long line of beautiful young female sports teachers who appear suddenly as part of their Teachers College training. She looks a bit like a blonde Barbie doll in a tracksuit, loaning out sports gear to kids at lunchtime. And she's always so happy and upbeat.

Some kids borrow sports gear just to perve at the way the tracksuit neatly hugs her body. A beautiful perfume wafts out as Sam and I grab a cricket ball, a metal wicket, pads, gloves, a box and a bat. We sign our names in the book.

'Thanks Miss,' I call out, but she doesn't notice.

There is a growing line of sweaty male teenagers with dishevelled hair who are taking up her time and attention. We stumble along carrying the gear, the way you do when you are overloaded. Half carrying, half dragging, and inspecting the pitch in the middle of the oval. There's comfort in pretending to face up to a bowler. Standing in front of the imaginary stumps. Sam runs in and pretends to bowl, appeals and follows through kicking 'the stumps' over. We pass girls sitting cross-legged who hold tight to their skirts and, when they stand, brush themselves down the way cats clean their fur.

They never play sport. They just talk. We jostle past the year eights playing their mini cricket matches next to the wire fence, and settle next to the nets.

Soon we're throwing the ball onto the slips cradle. It skims off at odd angles, then one slides straight on. The faster you throw, the quicker it comes off.

Once, it steeples so high it almost goes over the school fence. We take turns throwing red hard composition balls to each other in the nets. Sometimes it catches the bottom of the wire fencing, gathering speed as it goes. We jump out of the way to avoid it. Laughter booms after a painful knock on the shins.

'Stop laughing, you bastard.'

I'm lying on my back holding my knees to my chest. The siren sounds, and we wander back to the PE office. Mr Bawden, the middle-aged head of sport with black slicked-back hair, sorts through the returned gear.

'Don't dump it there, put it back properly.'

Then it's through the gates and across the road to try to get back to class before the second bell rings. We gather our books and walk into maths class with Mr Shepherd, a large bearded man whose deep mellifluous voice makes me think of the vanilla slices the school canteen sells. The ones with the pink icing. There'll be no classroom chatter in this class. I manage to grab a window seat, look at the clock, and take a deep breath. It's only two hours until cricket practice.

Dad meets Pauline at a TAFE course for divorced people.

'If you are still bitter and angry, this course can't help,' the lecturer warns. 'This is all about moving on and leaving the past behind.'

He's much happier now that Pauline is on the scene. She lightens his mood and gives him something to look forward to.

Dad rarely reveals his anger at Mum, despite acutely feeling it. For years he collects newspaper articles about divorce. His diary entries, written even thirty years after she left, reveal his true feelings. But meeting Pauline helps him move on from the bitterness that follows his divorce from Mum.

Pauline owns a small farm near McLaren Vale in the state's south. Every second weekend, they play golf and enjoy a meal together.

Her availability is limited though.

One evening, a remark hastens Dad's departure. No overnighter this time.

'I'm still in love with my ex-husband, I'm sorry.'

Dad gets up out of the couch, a comfy one in front of the fire that overlooks the valley, where you can see mist drifting on cold mornings.

I imagine his drive all the way back to Glen Osmond must have been a deflating one, turning his car down the steep driveway at Dutton Street, pulling up and then walking through the front door alone.

The relationship is put on the backburner, only to be ignited once in a while.

Sir Donald Bradman's large red-brick house sits next to Pembroke's senior school campus on Holden Street. Fig trees drop fruit on the school's quadrangle, making you look twice before sitting down on wooden benches sprinkled throughout. I never spot the Don and am more concerned about the lack of cricket nets at the new campus. There's also no sports shed. Bring your own gear or walk down the Parade to the middle school to borrow theirs. Most days I go to the library to read about cricket, mainly instructional manuals although there's the odd book about Test series in the 1960s.

A plane drifts across the Adelaide skyline and a mist hovers above the calm water. It's March 1979 and year eleven's a slog. Dad and I sit outside at a small round table on his balcony. I'm struggling with new subjects at school: Physics, Maths 1 and Maths 2.

'Don't worry I'll help,' Dad says. 'These subjects get marked up in Matric.'

But I don't understand the principles and Dad has trouble teaching things that come easily to him. He gets annoyed. His voice grows louder and more frustrated with my confusion.

'Did you listen to what I just said?'

I nod.

He's better at helping me with English.

I'm learning Macbeth's speech, the one about the player 'that struts and frets his hour upon the stage'.

'Hooray,' Dad says with a smile, raising his arms above his head as if he's a bowler appealing for a wicket.

I've just recited the full thirteen lines as afternoon shadows creep across us. But all this is irrelevant. I'm going to be opening the batting for Australia soon. That's what my classmates tell me.

When the school week ends, I roam the city. On Friday afternoons I meet up with mates at a record store in an arcade off the Rundle Mall, just part of the teenage throng that floods through with wayward hair, loose ties and unpolished shoes. That's how I learn the meaning of the word 'apocalypse'. From the soundtrack to Francis Ford Coppola's movie *Apocalypse Now*.

'It means the end of the world,' says Sam.

It's a movie about the Vietnam War. Where US soldiers take the canals, and cop the Viet Cong's bullets and spears. It opens with Martin Sheen going mad.

There's a routine to the visits to the record store. Lift the record out of the sleeve, study the cover. Ask the shop assistant to put on an album. Stand listening through headphones attached to the wall.

Whenever I go, I get lost in the sound. A feeling like facing a bowler in the nets.

A strong breeze blows across the deck of the ocean liner *Fairstar*.

Alan McGilvray's voice on crackling airwaves describes Kim Hughes being caught for 99 at the WACA. It's December 1979, day one of the Second Test of the revamped dual season of England and the West Indies, all televised on Channel Nine. Mum's taken me on a cruise around some of the Pacific Islands. Snorkelling for coral off Suva and Tonga, shopping in the markets at Fiji and Samoa. She provides a lesson in bartering. Perhaps she was reaching for happy memories of the *Oriana*. We play the pokies in gaudy-coloured lounges that reek of smoke. Mum declines the advances of a French sailor who massages her feet one night on the ship's deck. I spend my afternoons admiring oiled-up bikini-clad women lounging around the pool until Mum rounds me up for bingo.

A daily newsletter slides under the cabin door with snippets of international news. I wake to the sound of a loud foreign-sounding voice announcing the day's activities. The accent reminds me of the actor who played Inspector Poirot from the movie *Murder on the Orient Express*, which we'd seen as a family at the drive-in at West Beach.

We dock at Sydney at dawn after watching the lights of the city flicker like low-set stars. My return is dampened by the news I have failed year eleven.

10. Distractions · 1980

In class, Mr Smith describes the roar at the opening bounce of a VFL grand final as 'like a jumbo jet taking off'. His passion for sport is matched only by his love of literature. He is the one who convinces the headmistress that if I use a fountain pen to write I could do year twelve.

Studies, though, prove difficult. Steve is spinning out. He's divorcing from Bronwyn and living with Mum and staying up late playing records. Steve's lawyer visits. He's also Glenelg's former captain, Peter Marker. The encounter is brief. I note how much bigger Marker is in the flesh than he looked on the field during Sturt's 1974 grand final win.

Marker probably wonders what he's got himself in for.

Steve plays the stereo so loud some nights that I have trouble sleeping. He's in and out of work. Mum's beside herself with worry.

Steve's full of theories.

One day he pulls his car suddenly into Mum's drive, like I've seen the cops do on the TV show *Homicide*. I am out the front, playing in a new cricket bat, tapping an old ball on the freshly oiled bat.

Steve's a bit wide-eyed and panicked.

'What's the matter?' I ask.

'The number plates of other cars send me directions when I'm driving.'

'What do you mean?'

'The number plate UFM 17 means,' and then he pauses as if he's telling me some secret code, 'you follow me for seventeen kilometres.'

'But they'll think you're stalking them.'

He tells me how he only follows the instructions for a little while before another car sends him a message.

'Someone was just following me. So I'm not the only one doing it.'

The next day he rings me at Mum's.

'Barry, I just wanted you to know that you are a number nine. You should be safe.'

That is one of the unknowns. Will he ever be a threat to anyone other than himself?

I don't think so. But some days I'm not so sure.

Despite Mr Smith's enthusiasm I'm failing at school. I go down in three of out five subjects at the end of term two in year twelve, just before we break for the September holidays prior to exams.

I've failed three driving tests as well.

A bundle of nerves, I pass the ranking parking test then fail the release of a handbrake driving up a hill. It seems to me that each driving instructor is more grim-faced.

Steve comes through in more lucid moments. He suggests I take some driving lessons in his car, which is easier to handle than Dad's Cortina.

A few lessons and a pass. I whoop with joy.

'More confidence, that's what you needed,' says the

instructor as he signs the form to say I've passed.

Exam time, and David Bowie's on a roll. November 1980.

'Ashes to Ashes' plays in my head on continual rotation. It has a deep, dark and even hypnotic sound. The record won't stop. Just one more time in my mind.

My first solo drive is down the beach to cool my mind before the exams. The radio's blaring and the temperature is summer-Sunday-night hot. I drive to the esplanade and watch people taking their dogs for a walk. A layer of heat hangs over the city. At dusk I head back with sand stuck to my feet.

'Ashes to Ashes' has gone away.

We pile into the school hall. Nervous glances from students contrast with the expressionless examiner who sits out the front. A lack of air conditioning adds to the claustrophobic conditions.

'You may begin.'

Time seems to accelerate as the three hours moves toward an end.

Stretch, yawn.

'Ten minutes left,' says the examiner.

It's like batting in cricket. Some exams are easier than others. English, Modern European History and Economics are like playing on a truer pitch. Biology and Maths 1S are like struggling in bad light with a fast bowler pinging it around your ears. I flit back and forth between questions trying to find clarity of thought.

Then it's over.

After each exam, students spill chattering from the hall, the noise escalating with every step.

I walk out for the last time and it hits me like a cool breeze that I'll never have to go to school again.

George Benson's 'Give Me the Night' crackles out of the radio as I drive. But I am not sure where to go. I head up the Parade and take a left to head to Sam's house to see if he wants to come down to the nets for a hit. That's where I always go when I'm not sure where to go or what to do. Unless it's footy season. Then Sam and I go to the oval near Dad's for some end-to-end screw punts and talk about Woody Allen comedies.

But right now it's the start of summer holidays.

A slight haze rolls over Kangaroo Island, off the Fleurieu Peninsula, which I can see through the hotel window. I reach for my John Lennon T-shirt, the one with Lennon and his frizzy hair and round glasses and the word *Imagine* across the front. Australia is playing a one-dayer at the WACA. The TV shows a long view of the ground as Dad and I unpack our gear to the sound of Richie Benaud's voice.

There's something unfamiliar about an international cricket ground this day. Beatles music blares out of the loudspeakers. Richie in his beige coat has a serious look on his face.

'The reason you're hearing The Beatles is that news has come through that John Lennon has been shot dead in New York.'

Dad and I walk around the island. We look at the penguins and visit the bakery. Bite into a big slab of jam and cream in a Kitchener bun. Talking about what I'd like to do next year. It's father to son, a form of gentle masculinity that's rarely credited. It reminds me of the day paddling on the River Torrens.

Just after Christmas the postie arrives with my exam result. I've scored 333, enough to get into the physical education course at Teachers College.

The number three. Vera, who died in August, has been watching over me. Mum's all smiles and is the first to offer congratulations.

She brings in a chocolate cake covered in icing. Dad calls from work.

'Well done, Barry, that's a great result.'

Steve delivers a bottle of champagne. He takes photos around Mum's lounge-room table.

My highest mark was for Math 1S, the only subject that was marked up.

So the old boy was right all along.

The days that follow see an outpouring of emotion about the death of Lennon as songs from the album *Double Fantasy* fill the airwaves. Mum has marked up her book, *Peace from Nervous Suffering: A practical guide to understanding, confidence and recovery*, on the chapter that stresses a need to find a new way of looking at something that appears to be unresolvable.

Mum's also underlined sentences where author Dr Claire Weekes encourages kinder language. The word 'depletion' replaces 'depression' to remove stigma and encourage. Repletion can follow and so there is hope for recovery.

Much later, I discover that Dad was doing his own reading at this time, including a self-published book by Norm Barber called *How to have a Successful Nervous Breakdown in Adelaide*. Dad, with his background in science, is always looking for causes and reasons for Steve being the way he is.

As a family we're still looking for a solution to my eldest brother's tortured existence, but at least we can try to have some control over the effect it is having on us. We each go looking for distractions.

The moon throws a light over the silent river. It's just after dusk. The banks of the River Murray, late December 1982.

'Now, where were we?' she asks.

She's on top of me now and lowers her mouth. I'm grabbing tufts of grass next to the rug we're lying on. Even the moon looks different that night. But let's go back for a moment. It's Boxing Day and we're driving up the highway past the tollgate and through the Adelaide Hills. Greg and Gary are leading the way in their new two-door Scorpion. Low to the ground. The convoy of young men in cars is heading to Mannum, eighty-four kilometres east of Adelaide.

The trip means independence, beer, loud music and a glass-smooth river. Walkmans, mullets, acid-wash jeans, perms, brown leather jackets, Reebok sneakers, sleeveless T-shirts and Ansell condoms in the overcooked glove boxes of our cars, just in case. We gather by our tents near the river. We scoff what is left of the potato chips and skol cans of beer like teenagers can, knowing it won't make any difference to our weight. Our bodies are lean and muscular and supple. The next day cricket commentary tumbles out of the radio.

The sound seeps down the river as the delayed reactions of voices in shacks bounce off the water's surface.

'What's the score?'

We exist in that twilight zone between teenage years and manhood that can last for decades. As we ski, drink and talk, the Boxing Day Test match of 1982/83 continues to sway. David Hookes is scoring runs. At last it looks like he'll become a more permanent member of the Australian team. We're invested in Hookesy. He's a Croweater like us.

Early starts, late finishes. Wisdoms are shared, or at least that's what we think they are.

A few days in, young women appear. They lie on deckchairs in the house next door. It is like finding a lost tribe. Gary is sent out as an emissary to make contact.

'Great news,' he says with a smile as if he's just won the lottery. 'They've just asked us to a party. Powder up, boys.'

It's either talcum powder or a spray of Brut 33, although Blue Stratos is also popular. A timer is placed next to the shower and it's not for concerns over the environment. We go as one to the party.

Eight ball is played. Phil Collins' 'In the Air Tonight' rises over the nervous chatter. We stand arms folded, like we do at the cricket club. Beer held just in front of the left bicep.

'Wanna game?'

A lean pretty girl with tight light-blue pants hands me the pool cue. She has a street savviness I lack.

She wins easily in a matter of minutes, smiling as she pots each ball. 'Don't like losing to a girl, hey?' Delivered with a flirtatious grin.

Part drunk, part excited, our group stumbles back to our cars, leaving the party behind. I've been relegated to where the luggage is normally stored. As we're about to drive she appears.

'Hey, wait for me.'

She jumps in the back, hurling her chewing gum out the window. It's just me and the eight-ball champ in the back of the car. Her hand finds mine and squeezes it. We kiss and fumble around on the journey home before she bids me farewell with a kiss.

'See ya later.'

That night I learn the meaning of blue balls.

The next day the girls have disappeared.

'Gone home,' the owner of the shack tells us. A sense of

gloom descends on the camp, just like you feel when you get a first ball duck.

Then a miracle. The night before we head back to Adelaide, she's leaning on the wire fence with her entourage of girlfriends.

'We're heading down the park, wanna come?' she says, holding a picnic basket.

Soon we're all walking. A gang of ten. We approach the park where the *Murray River Queen* sits.

'Come this way,' she says with a wink.

We peel away from the group into the darkness. The moon in all its brightness leads a path of light reflecting off the river as if it is guiding the way.

We roll up tents and pack the cars. Gary, Greg and I are lying in the lounge inside the shack. The trip is wearing thin. We speak to each other in dismissive tones with croaky comments. Pillow fights no longer end well.

The final day of the MCG Test is on the radio and TV. It could be over in one ball. Australia needs 292 to win but has collapsed at 9 for 218 by the time Jeff Thomson arrives late on the fourth day.

Allan Border is in the middle of the MCG trying to regain form by taking singles. I watched him the week before at the Adelaide Oval struggle his way to 26 off 95 balls in more than two hours.

In 1982/83, the never-say-die left-hander who became one of Australian cricket's most valuable assets looked like someone who couldn't strike a break. Border, who rose from the ashes of the battle between the Establishment and World Series Cricket, and made it into the full-strength side under

Greg Chappell. Border, who came two runs close to back-to-back tons against the might of the West Indies in 1984.

Border, who became a byword for respect.

But in this series he's on the verge of being dropped.

Then in the Melbourne Test, Bob Willis, England's skipper, late on the fourth afternoon allows Border to rotate the strike with ease trying to get to the tail-enders. At stumps he's on 44 and Thomson 8.

Day five, the MCG gates opened for free. There are almost 20,000 clapping and cheering each ball as Australia moves closer to the target. We watch on a small black-and-white screen. The reception fails, and Greg jumps up and stands with his hand on the antenna.

'That ok?'

'Not yet. Stay there though.'

'Well then, you bastards do it.'

The camera peers into the Australian dressing room. The usually unflappable Greg Chappell stands at the back looking nervous. Kim Hughes, wearing an Australian jumper with a lighter shade of green, tosses a cricket ball from one hand to the other. England fieldsmen start to panic as Border makes it to 50 and Australia closes in on the target. Then it happens.

Botham is thrown the ball. He bounds in. Drops one just short of a length and Thommo nicks to Tavaré who looks like he's half asleep at slip. The ball rebounds to Geoff Miller, who catches it.

A collective groan is heard across the country including in a small shack in Mannum. The Poms run from the field triumphant.

But Allan Border is back, just when the critics are saying he's finished.

It's March 1983 when Bob Hawke leads Labor to victory in the Federal election. The one that freshly deposed leader Bill Hayden said the drover's dog could have won. I'd heard about Hawke, when as the head of the ACTU, he helped convince Bradman and the Board to cancel South Africa's tour of Australia in 1971/72. That summer Mum took me to the Adelaide Oval to watch Garry Sobers, but I had to settle for a treat from the canteen beneath the grandstand when the match finished early.

Election night, Dad and I watch the broadcast from the Canberra tally room on a colour television in his lounge room. Dad explains unfamiliar words from commentators' mouths. Bellwether seat, a four percent swing, and exit polls. A Golden Chicken hot pack with gravy, potato and peas in an alfoil dish sits on trays in our laps. On the tele, Hawke, the 'silver bodgie', pokes his head around the tally room corner, then he and Hazel walk on stage. The newly elected prime minister looks like he can't wait to start running the country as Hazel's eyes dart nervously around. The ABC's Richard Morecroft perches on an elevated desk next to a moustachioed Barrie Cassidy. Analog clocks line the wall showing different time zones in various states and territories. Malcolm Fraser has already appeared, showing rare emotion. His bottom lip quivers and he has trouble getting words out conceding defeat. I know that feeling. It's how I feel when I am dismissed for a low score, like I had been earlier that day when we had to bat just twenty minutes before stumps. But it's Hawke's night and a new political era has begun.

I don't know exactly when Dorothy arrives on the scene but she's a charismatic Scot, a force of nature so different to Mum that I figure Dad and Dorothy will get along well.

She sweeps through tennis days and lunches, organising everyone like Julie Andrews in *The Sound of Music*. She's a radiographer and a former gardening correspondent at the BBC who exudes positivity.

They have an old-fashioned relationship. Dad pays for most things, including dinners out. They holiday on the Sunshine Coast, in Bali, take sailing and houseboat trips, and travel to the Riverland once a year for a week of golf.

She sits back, smiles and entertains while Dad looks on. Dorothy is persuasive in everything she does and it's no surprise when she later becomes a real estate agent.

I'm pleased for Les as he seems more confident and content with Dorothy in his life. Although Dad has real affection for her, he remains in his own way unreachable. When Dot pushes for more, Dad can't provide it.

Eccentricities run in families, like underwater streams. Some days they burst to the surface. My dad's paternal uncle Leo was a hoarder. When he died they found every room but one in the house full of newspapers piled to the ceiling. He probably had a greater archive than the State Library.

Leo worked as a packer for the *Adelaide News*, loading papers onto trucks to be transported across the state.

We are all a bit like that in my family. All a little bit obsessive. We are also thorough, just like Leo.

Leo was a bachelor. 'He had a lady friend,' Dad added whenever we spoke of Leo, as if to ward off any questions.

Leo loved bushwalking. He left $30,000 to the Field Naturalists Society of South Australia in 1971. They banked it, earned money on the interest and watched it grow.

A decade later they bought some land in the Pohlner Estate, eighty kilometres north-east of Adelaide in the Mount Lofty Ranges of the Kaiserstuhl Conservation Park.

In January 1983, we gather to honour Leo's contribution. A row of chairs sits on a dry patch of dirt. Flies pester, and the summer temperature rises. Sweat forms under our armpits. The state environment minister, Don Hopgood, looks dapper in his grey suit. He's making a speech about Leo's donation and talks with the polish of someone used to an audience.

A short round of applause. Then a silence, a cooling breeze. Dad walks to the rostrum and starts filling in the details of Leo's life. The rostrum is one of those high ones where you have to climb some steps. The wind almost scatters Dad's notes and the microphone exacerbates any little fumbles.

'Leo Wakem was one of four sons of Edwin and Sarah Nicholls. His antecedents were typical of South Australia in the eighteen nineties.' Then he talks about the history of the land. 'The park's name was changed during the First World War to Mount Kitchener as part of the anti-German sentiment.'

Dad's speech is full of research and details. He sounds nervous, like the role is unfamiliar. He's been working on the family history dating back to the members of the Nicholls clan, miners from Cornwall, who arrived in South Australia not long after settlement.

Afterwards we share polite conversation and morning tea.

'Pity there's no plaque,' Dad says as we drive away down the dusty road.

He writes a letter to the minister, thanking him for his

contribution and expressing some disappointment at nothing 'official' on site.

Some months later we go back for another ceremony. Dad takes a photo of me leaning on a fence. I'm nineteen and as lean as a rake. I have the naïve smile of a teenager. Dad's standing next to a plaque acknowledging Leo's contribution.

He has the look of a minor success. The plaque is dedicated to the memory of Leo Wakem Nicholls (1894–1971) described as a 'keen bushwalker'.

Later the SA Field Naturalists Society give Leo a mention in their annual report, describing Leo Wakem Nicholls as:

> a very tight-lipped man who never spoke about his personal affairs ... in his later years he became untidy, ill kept and dressed shabbily. It also appears during this period until his death he was content to live on scraps and water. This man apparently did not make friends easily and was unapproachable. He possibly led a lonely and sad life on normal standards and in his latter years had only one friend. Mr Nicholls joined the society in 1948 and the records show that his membership lapsed after 1953. He must, however, have retained his interest in the society because of the bequest made under his will in 1954.

Dad rips the page out in disgust. I wonder what they would have written about Leo if he'd donated less.

11. Holidays • 1984–85/2015

Families in four-wheel drives roar into town in that 'fuck off I'm coming through' type of way. It's Easter 2015 and kids squabble in back seats watching DVDs. Busselton's population swells by three times. City-dwellers arrive for their long weekend at familiar holiday haunts. I've taken a right turn just before the foreshore, past beach houses where shirtless men and young women in bikinis sit on the balconies in two-storey beach houses. Towels hang from the railings as if marking out territory. Excited voices carry while colours blaze like a surfing photo from California in the 1960s. The autumn light has not yet begun to fade. I park behind a sand dune. The sound of waves washing to shore rolls over me.

The next day I'm awake at dawn in a hit of sunlight and anxiety. The gym is alive. Smack bang into an early morning cardio class. More nightclub sound than the clinking of weights. The instructor shouts encouragement.

The noise goes right through me. My mind races. I ride, I run, I lift weights. I try everything I can to get a sweat up. Nothing works, so I drive to a local picket-ringed oval next to the beach. People are already up making the most of the last gasp of warm weather. A sunlit day has boats out early, and young families meandering along the foreshore. In an intuitive move, I wander to the centre of the oval.

I haven't played cricket for years, but it provides comfort. I ring Dad and speak to him. I'm walking in circles feeling distressed. I call Dr Best. He offers to send a script to a local chemist to help me get through the weekend. But then we realise it's Good Friday.

'I think you need to go to ED to get a small dose just to calm you down.'

I curse myself for not being outside enjoying the day with my family. But that's part of all of this. The beating yourself up. I could have been down the beach with Ann and my kids, jumping off the jetty, watching them in the playground, having an ice-cream, anything but sitting in the ED of a hospital.

I eventually get seen by the doctor, who is empathetic. He gives me some benzo. I take the chill pill and, the next day, pick up the script.

The days feel long. Like they will never end. I can't wait to get back to work as a distraction.

1984. A week before Christmas a storm is brewing at home, but hits more like a full-force gale.

One night Mum asks me to stay at her house. Steve is psychotic. She doesn't feel safe in her own home. Maybe she figures because I am bigger than him, even though Steve is stronger, I will be able to cope if things get out of hand.

I agree to come over later and then head off to play cricket. It's a day where all the failures and frustrations of the past are made up for.

I'm dropped on nought at deep fine leg but then bat all day.

Dad and Steve come to watch and then walk around the oval

like two lost souls. Steve shuffles along like a zombie because of the medication. He encroaches on the ground and when the umpire approaches Steve raises his hands to apologise, realising the error he's made.

Laughter fills the air.

'Who's the spaceman?' one of my team mates calls out.

'Tone it down fellas,' one of them says, loud enough for me to hear.

Suddenly they fall silent. They have worked out what is going on.

They leave not long after. Dad waves at me as I watch him reverse his car out the Adelaide Oval car park and wonder where they are going.

After play, it's all beers and pats on the back from old-timers at the club but I don't stay for long.

That night, Mum sleeps over at Dad's – a sign of how fraught things have become. Steve seems ok but doesn't say much apart from telling me 'mental illness is the bargain basement of discrimination'.

Whenever he goes to the deli to buy smokes, the pub for a beer, or even the servo to fill up his car, people look at him like they think he's beneath them.

I settle into one of Mum's small spare bedrooms and drift off to sleep after watching some TV. I slip into a black void, not my usual sleep after scoring runs when I replay parts of the innings in my dreams.

At dawn, the sudden loud noise of a record being played disturbs me.

The stereo in Steve's room is on full volume. I'm partway through the door before he propels me into the drum kit next to the bedroom mirror.

I'm not injured, just shocked. I push back against him.

'What the fuck are you doing?'

He becomes aware of what he has done.

'Sorry, sorry, stay, you don't have to leave.'

I gather my clothes and head to Dad's house but it's another day of just coping. My family is lost. We don't know what to do or who to turn to. All I know is that Dad says under no circumstances am I to call the police. He doesn't want his son going to jail.

I'm on edge even more than before.

Adelaide is about to be nuked.

Steve speaks like the character Michael Douglas plays in *The China Syndrome*, who's trying to convince the owners of a meltdown at a nuclear power station.

'We've got to get out of Adelaide, it's not safe for anyone,' he says as his eyes dart from side to side. The threat he's expressed is very real. To him.

My car's parked in Mum's driveway, which sweeps up past her backyard with lemon trees and shrubs.

'Move your car,' he screams. 'If you don't, I'm going to reverse into it.'

Steve's buzzing around the lounge room, talking about how dangerous it is living in Australia 'in the current environment'. He's stressing that we all need to go to the desert.

'You're not talking sense,' I say.

His eyes display a rare moment of clarity, like a switch has been flicked. 'Yes of course, you are right.' But then he swings back in an instant. 'Move your fucking car.'

As I get into my car, he already has the engine going. I reverse, with Steve not far in front of me, reversing his. We reach the end of the driveway as he screeches his wheels and heads down the road.

I watch the SWAT team jump the fence of my mum's neighbour's house loaded with guns and know the situation has escalated. I am looking through the kitchen window, on the phone to my girlfriend Glenda.

'Just hold on a second.'

Glenda's pretty, effervescent, intelligent, perceptive and very sensitive. Maybe too sensitive, for me at any rate. She's close to Steve in a sisterly way. They chat, and smoke on Mum's back verandah where Glenda spends more time than at her own home. Glenda's quit university but she doesn't want her parents to know. So, she catches two buses every day to my mum's place, to pretend she's doing the second year of her science degree.

But Glenda's not here this morning. We've had a row. Another one. Birds wash in the small bath in the middle of the lawn. Then there's the interruption.

Police sirens pierce the air as the men arrive.

'I'll have to call you back,' I tell Glenda.

'Is everything ok? Call me when you get the ...'

Glenda's voice on the end of the line trails off as I put the receiver down.

I lean closer to the window.

For this to make any sense, you need to know what just unfolded.

Steve has fallen prey to opportunistic scum. Mum's neighbour is a six-foot twenty-something with a handlebar moustache and foreign accent who wears reflective glasses. He and his two young housemates walk around as if they own the street. They've seen Steve in his psychotic state, and the CB radios that Steve sometimes leaves in his car. Steve has bought the CBs off a friend from church and now he's put them in the paper for sale again. Mum's next-door neighbour has seen the adverts, noted the address and joined the dots. They've concocted a plan. But there's a problem. Steve and his radios are at Dad's house, not my mother's.

There's an urgent knock at Mum's door. An unfamiliar shadow lurks behind the glass. I go to unlock it but he's barging in, or at least trying to.

'Hey, hold on!'

'I'm Detective Burns from the Norwood CIB and your brother Steve has stolen my CB radios. Where can I find him? This is very urgent.'

'Wait there.' I shut him out again. Everything about this bloke looks wrong. A policeman dressed in tennis whites and sandshoes? I feel confused and a little intimidated. Since when did the next-door neighbour become a cop?

I ring Dad.

'Put him on the phone, Barry.'

I let the man in and hand him the phone. Dad tells him to bring police ID and is immediately suspicious when he asks my dad how to get to Glen Osmond, the suburb just a few kilometres away from Mum's.

The 'detective' heads off to my father's house while Dad calls the Norwood Police Station and police headquarters in Angas Street.

'There's no Detective Burns working here,' they tell him.

An orange station wagon arrives at Dad's house. We later

find out that it's from a motor dealer's yard on a test drive.

Dad's watching from inside as the visitor paces up and down, speaking into a walkie-talkie. The 'detective' is making a scene to alert the neighbours that there's a problem.

Dad locks all the doors and heads to the front lawn.

'I want you to take me inside to see the radios which were advertised for sale,' the man says.

Dad asks for his police identification.

'I haven't got it with me,' the 'detective' says, looking in his wallet and inadvertently revealing a uni photo ID.

'Which police station are you based at?' Dad asks.

'I've had my ID stolen and I'm based interstate.' He's shouting now. 'If you don't let me in I will call a blue car!'

'If you don't show me your ID I'll be the one calling the blue car.'

Dad knows the significance of an ID. He's a senior manager at WRE and has to show his pass before he is allowed through the gates each day. Les also has a good bullshit detector and after the bloke has gone, he reports the matter to police, telling them where they can find him.

'It's the next-door neighbour of my ex-wife, northern side.'

Les calls me to describe what has happened and tells me under no circumstances am I to engage further with the man pretending to be a detective.

A few minutes later from Mum's kitchen, I see the SWAT team jumping the neighbour's fence.

There are always those who will try to take advantage of the marginalised in society. The ones who should be protected most. Mum's neighbour is just another example of how low some people will go.

The neighbour is charged with impersonating a police officer. In court, the defence lawyer tries a series of dirty tricks to cast my parents in a suspicious light.

'Has your ex-husband ever beat you up, Mrs Nicholls?'

'No.'

He tries to make it look like Dad and Mum collaborated on the day of the trial to invent a story. He's at Dad now, probing.

'Have you and your ex-wife spoken today?'

'Yes, we discussed the best place to park close to the courts.'

'Is it not true that you did not notice that your son stole my client's CB radios?'

Dad pauses. 'I've worked at WRE for the last thirty-five years. Communication must be as transparent as possible. We make a point of avoiding using double negatives.'

The lawyer tries to depict Dad as a fearful person locking his doors.

'But your client had a walkie-talkie,' Dad says. His implication is clear. There could have been two of them with conspiracy to commit a crime.

The police impersonator is found guilty and fined.

The incident is filed into family folklore.

Steve is right: mental illness is the fucking bargain basement of discrimination.

Christmas Day arrives like a mini earthquake.

'C'mon, time to open the presents,' says Mum.

Presents are exchanged, although it's tense and doesn't feel much like the festive season. Mum, Nanna, me and a mate of Steve's called Andy from the local church sit on chairs in the lounge room. Andy is in his thirties but has the sense of someone who is not yet ready to grow up. He wears a flannelette shirt, jeans and sandshoes and sometimes works in Mum's garden.

Family photos of happier times in England look on from picture frames.

Steve's busy making odd remarks and laughing, at times a little too boisterously. The rest of us exchange uncomfortable glances.

He's soon on the move between Mum's couch and the outdoor swing, smoking. Fag to mouth, deep inhale, twirl the hair, fag to mouth. It's torturous just watching him. He can't sit still.

'I'm just going for a drive. I need some more cigarettes.'

He spends most of his welfare money on fags and video hire. Six dollars for one new VHS release and five weeklies. Smoking, drinking and watching videos are the only things that calm Steve down. Better than any medication.

Once he leaves, we all exhale with relief. Half an hour goes by, then an hour.

'Maybe he just wants some time to himself,' says Nanna.

Mum's looking worried.

Steve's gone for a drive all right, and doesn't come back. Not in one hour, two hours, three hours. We eat our Christmas lunch in close to silence. It's no surprise he doesn't want to join in. He's had another year of being unemployed and lying around doing nothing. He's quit jobs at the drop of a hat. Quit one because someone else resigned. He's looking for reasons to leave work.

It's hard to distinguish between his depression and his laziness. Many days he doesn't bother getting out of bed.

By teatime Dad phones back with news.

Steve's called Dad from somewhere out on the Nullarbor

Plain. Dad pays the petrol station and asks Steve for a guarantee he'll use it to drive back.

'Yeah I promise.'

But I know what he's doing. He's going to the desert. Steve still thinks South Australia is about to have a nuclear bomb dropped on it.

The next day Dad tells me my eldest brother has reached the WA border. Dad again accepts responsibility of payment for the petrol station owner and Steve keeps driving.

He pulls the same trick four days in a row. I don't know where he sleeps, maybe in the car, but he's in one hell of a hurry.

Dad is just about pulling his hair out.

Mum and Dad talk to each other more now than when they were married.

Steve ends up in the psychiatric ward of the Kalgoorlie Hospital after a Salvation Army officer finds him wandering the streets. A month later, with his car on the train to Adelaide, Steve returns, seemingly much calmer. He's had a long bus trip back.

'The girl in the room next door broke the window and slit her wrists with the glass and died. I was glad to get out of the place.'

His fear of a nuclear holocaust has somehow passed.

Margaret and Les always donate to the Salvos whenever they see a member rattling their tin.

Mum and Dad are in Steve's psychiatrist's office.

'Your son has a serious mental illness.'

The assessment is eminently fair and his manner one of warmth and empathy.

My parents take some convincing. It's not easy to acknowledge that your son has a life-threatening illness, especially in the 1980s when mental health is heavily stigmatised.

Second-generation anti-psychotic drugs and anti-depressants are on the market, but less is known about their effectiveness or side effects. Steve is medicated to the eyeballs and at various times is prescribed lithium, Parnate, Prothiaden, and Mellaril. He barely resembles the person I once knew.

He'd disappeared like someone walking into the fog. His moods fluctuate wildly. Some days the side effects of the drugs are so bad he shakes like a Parkinson's patient. We are all in a holding pattern.

I don't know how Mum and Dad managed. Or how I coped. But maybe I didn't.

12. Consequences • 1985–86/2015

It feels like I can almost read the sea. The Bunbury Lighthouse stands sentry to the Indian Ocean. I sit in my car. There is a hotel with large glass windows behind me. Shadows move within as waiters ferry food between tables. The warmth of summer rays oozes through the windscreen. The car park is full of ocean watchers. Some stare at their phones. Others look straight ahead, lost in thought.

Cars rarely park in front of the grey rectangular bin that sits halfway along the angled parking. They pull in, see the obstructed view, and pull out again, like a dance choreography or a Benny Hill sketch.

What brings them here?

On the concrete path students from the local high school run past laughing, talking, gasping for air on the incline.

A phys ed teacher jogs on the spot.

'C'mon keep going,' she says, 'not far to go.'

She's urging them; ordering but also encouraging. It's like the military without the machismo. I was a phys ed teacher once, long ago.

It's a time I now barely relate to, before journalism, before having four kids, before this. Now I concentrate on getting lost and try to lose myself in the vastness of the ocean, as if it could swallow me up. It's as close to mindfulness as I can get.

I take a photo of the sea and post it on Facebook to try to make life look normal. Wind down the window and feel the rush of the breeze on my face, one of the few sensations I'm open to. The list is diminishing like raindrops dissipating on the windscreen.

I take out the plastic container of tuna and rice and a few crackers. Hunger is another sensation that's disappeared. All too soon the break is over. I drive down the main street of Bunbury, past The Rose Hotel and the bookstore I used to visit at lunchtime when my mind was still.

The radio springs back to life. Cold Chisel belts out a tune.

My mind is racing; I take a benzo just to slow my thoughts. I do this when my mind is scattered, blown into a thousand pieces. Hum 'Sweet Child o' Mine' by Guns N' Roses and let the pill dissolve in my mouth. The wave of relaxation is almost immediate. I can feel my thoughts slowing with every breath. I can coast along. Drift. A lightness of being.

Sweat drips from my brow as I lug my cricket kit over my shoulder and open the door to Mum's house. Pad straps fall over the broken zip. I call out. There's no answer so I walk through the house. Steve's there in his bedroom lying on his back next to a bottle of empty pills.

I call an ambulance. When it arrives, the medicos carry him out on a stretcher. Steve tries to say something to me, slightly raising his head, but he's barely conscious. I follow them to the hospital and wait. I find a public phone and call one of my team mates.

'I might miss the warm-up before the game. Can you tell the coach?'

I don't say why.

Eventually I am allowed into his hospital room.

'Why did you call the ambulance?' Steve snarls at me.

My girlfriend arrives on the steps of the hospital bailing me up to tell me how offended she is at something I said.

'It's not about you this time, Glenda.'

I'd had a gutful of the lot of them. Anger and frustration swells in me but it's hard to know who to blame, so I push my feelings down deeper.

An hour later I'm at Campbelltown Memorial Oval for the first match of the season.

'This is going to be your year,' the coach told me the Thursday night before the game.

There was a mix of first-class players and a few younger ones vying for a place in the Kensington A Grade. They are largely sourced from private schools in Adelaide, and the club is wrongly perceived as being too soft. Not able to win games when it matters.

It's match day but I don't feel up to it. My mind is in a fog. The last thing I want to do is open the batting in a game of A Grade district cricket.

I ask my coach for a quiet word. My head is still spinning. 'I don't feel comfortable opening the batting, can you drop me down the order?'

The coach nods and doesn't ask why. I don't tell him. He tells the captain. No one says anything. My team mates know I am supposed to be opening but, in their eyes, I've squibbed. I watch from the balcony all day, feeling ashamed.

One of our openers goes in and gets out first ball, then sits down and starts chatting as if nothing has happened. He's seen and played enough to know a first ball duck is just part of the game.

The middle order stabilises, and we bat all day and I don't even get a hit. The next day I am made to field at deep fine leg all afternoon. It is a tactic used to highlight that a player is on the outer. We bat in the second innings. I hit a boundary and then am out caught behind slashing at a wide delivery. I walk crestfallen off the ground. I feel like a failure and like I've missed another opportunity.

But I can't tell anyone about what's happening with Steve.

Twilight's approaching. Summer has forgotten its seasonal schedule. Darkness looms and there's an unfamiliar heat and humidity in the air. Players stay at training longer. There are no excuses for late arrivals.

John, the A grade coach, walks toward me. It's the week of the grand final.

He's short and stocky, wearing dark sunglasses and a salesman's smile. When he speaks, his head wobbles like a David Boon doll. He is in his early forties, but to me he's just another of those older men at the club who casts judgement and influence over which direction your cricket career might take.

John never gets angry, but his eyes narrow slightly if the news is bad.

Earlier that summer we'd chatted over a beer after I'd thrown my wicket away in my 40s just before the drinks break. I'd batted through difficult times on a seaming wicket against the Yorkshire County import, Peter Hartley, who was jagging the ball around easily removing our top and middle order.

West Indian great Gordon Greenidge stood in the slips,

arms folded, watching on with an amused expression, while former Indian opener Chetan Chauhan crouched in the gully.

'Here's a beer,' John said with a smile as he handed me a schooner. This was the soft sell. The hard sell would come later. 'That was pretty tough out there today. You made a good forty, Bazza, you looked the part out there. A real A grader.' He sipped his beer and motioned me to do the same. 'But you blew a chance to make a big score. You had the chance to make a name for yourself, really establish yourself in the number three position against quality opposition. But you blew it by throwing your wicket away.'

He took another sip, waiting for my response. I just nodded and listened although I was quietly annoyed.

But he was right. I'd got myself out when I was set, and exposed a new batsman to a bowling attack that was already on top.

'I could see you losing concentration during the over.'

I didn't want to tell him that I lost concentration as I was so mentally fagged because of the anxiety I sometimes felt. So I said nothing.

When the grand final arrives in March of 1986, errors like that are remembered.

'Sorry, Baz, but you won't be playing.'

I watch Kensington coast to victory at Adelaide Oval, sitting in front of the dressing room knowing I'd helped them get to the finals.

'Come up and sit with us.' It is John the coach.

But it doesn't feel right sitting in the dressing room with the players.

They take the premiership photo on the weekend after the

grand final. I am not even invited. I leave the club before the next season starts.

It was the right decision to drop me. I was an anxious starter and I had trouble rotating the strike. Pressure tended to build on the team the longer I batted when it should have been easing. Sometimes hard decisions need to be made.

I feel defeated by anxiety.

Again.

The worse I feel, the slower time moves. Or that is the way it seems. Some days it's like falling down a deep well or trying to play a bouncer that has suddenly 'gotten big' on you. You can't escape it.

It doesn't help that depression is one of those anomalies in medical treatment – it can take six weeks or more for medication to begin to work, if it does at all.

The tablets can make you feel worse. Then you need stronger drugs because you feel so ill, like a vicious cycle.

I know how it feels when antidepressants work. Thoughts slow, anxiety recedes, thinking is clearer and energy levels are high. Creativity flourishes and optimism abounds. Nothing appears insurmountable.

I'd been on and off them for about ten years when Dr Best changed my script after I'd had some failing eyesight. Then I'd lowered the dose of the new one before taking myself off it all together.

I was sick of them. I was sick of the weight gain, the reduced libido and general lethargy that came with longer-term use. It had got to the point where I didn't think it was making much of a difference.

But this time nothing's working.

'So how are you today, Barry?' asks Dr Goria.

'Struggling, to be honest.'

Struggling. That was the word I'd say to team mates if I was having trouble scoring runs.

'Tell me exactly how you've been feeling.'

He listens and when I stop, he pauses, puts his notes to one side.

'Look, you're good at painting a picture in words. I hear you do it every day on the radio. Now try to picture this. At the moment you are in a speeding car going down a hill. I know this is hard for you, but you need to stop and get out of the car.' He repeats the image to emphasise the point and stands up. 'You need to stop the car, get out and walk away from it. This is very important that you do this. We need to give your brain a rest.'

He is right, and I know it but I just can't do it. My mind continues to race. I persist in seeking out information on the internet, my foot firmly on the accelerator.

You can barely see it from where I'm standing at the oval's edge. The coin tumbles in the air, beginning the arc that helps determine the fate of twenty-two players waiting nervously for the outcome. Two men stand in the middle of the light-brown pitch. Time slows as we wait for the captain to decide.

A shadow stroke means we are batting, and a small circular movement of the arm means we are in the field.

The gnawing anxiety spills to exhaustion if you can't stop it. But with cricket and anxiety there is always a natural end. You're either in the field, score runs or miss out.

Real life is different.

The captains chat for what seems to be a long time, then

ours makes a movement with his arm. We are in the field.

Anxiety disappears as excitement builds. For now.

I'm with my mate Paul from my new cricket club and the bloke on stage at Adelaide's Memorial Drive is screaming. The sound bursts from the stage. Sweat- and liquor-soaked Jimmy Barnes punches out the song 'Cheap Wine'. The end of a red bandana swings from his head as he swigs another drink from a flagon of gin. His is a raw, crude energy. He must be off his face, but the crowd doesn't care. In fact, we all celebrate it.

The smell of marijuana drifts in as the mob sings out of time with the music. Girls sit on blokes' shoulders, strangers talk and hug one another.

Paul and I soak up the atmosphere. He's a few years older and built like a twig. We open the batting for Tea Tree Gully. I'm the grafter in the partnership. Paul is full of class. He works as a car salesman and has the gift of the gab. He's good enough to play for South Australia but is a little different in personality to the macho style of the state cricket team. Paul's slightly awkward socially and speaks his mind. He also drinks Coke not beer, so is held in some quarters in suspicion. And he doesn't fit into the hierarchical culture. He questions authority. Team players supposedly aren't supposed to do that. A few seasons earlier, Paul was twelfth man for New South Wales, a team that included Steve and Mark Waugh.

He's also a fine captain who leads by example and really can bat.

That's the way we talk at cricket clubs. A person 'can play' or 'can bat'. It's the ultimate compliment. Paul glides into his strokes as if he is making little effort. He has plenty of time to play his shots. The ball speeds to the boundary with ease.

It's all about timing, technique and temperament. He's rarely flustered.

Paul scores his runs quickly too. He just keeps the score ticking over. You barely notice the scoreboard moving and then you look up and he's 50 not out.

Most days I just push the ball around the field hoping to hit one in the middle. Only some days do I bat like I can in the nets. When I move freely without a care in the world.

We sit together in the dressing room as I nervously jiggle my cricket sprigs up and down on the concrete floor. Paul can sense my nerves.

'It's time to face the music, Baz.'

No matter how bad you feel, eventually you need to face up to life and the responsibilities that come with it. Like facing the opening bowlers. The pitch is an unknown, the ball is new and swings. You don't know what will be delivered, and it can be a lonely space. It's easy to overthink.

I wait as the bowler and ten fieldsmen move into position.

'C'mon, let's knock him over, he doesn't look comfortable out here.'

I mark guard, middle and leg, look around the field trying to block out the sound of the opposition's chat that echoes around the ground. The umpire looks up.

'Play.'

Then silence. I look down at the white markings on the crease and wait. I hope it will be a good day.

November 1987. Reliance World Cup Final, with adverts plastered across Indian billboards. A hot Sunday morning in Australia.

It's even hotter in the middle of Eden Gardens, Calcutta, where close to 100,000 watch Australia play England. The images look distant and the TV footage occasionally jumps. Commentators sound like they are broadcasting from an echo chamber.

My old team mate Tim May is playing for Australia; my friend Richard Moody's brother Tom is in the touring squad. Mike Veletta, who I'd met on a night out with Richard in Perth plays a pivotal role.

'We work hard, don't we mate?' Veletta told me at the bar. 'And we play hard.' He raised a glass.

He was standing next to future Australian wicketkeeper Tim Zoehrer who'd also spent the day playing in a state trial in the early spring heat.

They'd all kicked on with their careers and I was treading water, thinking about quitting grade cricket.

In the World Cup Final, Veletta plays a crucial role scoring a breezy 45 off 31 balls to finish off Australia's innings of 5 for 253.

He performs above himself with a nimble-footed display to John Emburey and Eddie Hemmings. Phil DeFreitas opens the bowling for England. A few seasons earlier he'd made the ball bounce and zing off the Adelaide grade pitches.

McDermott, with a white sweatband on his left hand, traps England's opener Tim Robinson in front first ball of the innings. England has the chase under control when Mike Gatting plays a reverse sweep off Allan Border and scoops to Greg Dyer's gloves.

DeFreitas belts May around Eden Gardens. Steve Waugh bowls a crucial over that swings the momentum back. McDermott delivers the last ball. Tail-ender Neil Foster squirts the ball to the deep cover boundary where Veletta picks up and throws it back to Greg Dyer.

Australia wins by seven runs.

Border sits on the shoulders of his team mates, completing a victory lap. Australia wasn't expected to get into the finals, let alone win the championship.

In a time of great doubt from cricket fans, Australia had faced the music and won. The scene was set for a comeback after several years on the periphery.

13. Deeper into the darkness · 1988/2015

There's a deep, dark well and it feels like I'm diving to the bottom of it. There are days when I wonder if I am morphing into Steve on some predestined course.

Steve, who spent hours sitting outside at Mum's house on the swing on her back patio, chain-smoking, ruminating and fiddling with his hair, which was falling out. I'd ask him what was wrong. He'd stare straight ahead as if trying to finish a sentence in his mind before he spoke.

'You know those merry-go-rounds where kids jump on and make it spin faster? Well, that's what it's like with my thoughts. They just keep speeding up and it's hard to get off the merry-go-round.'

Dr Goria is talking to me about the next drug he wants to try.

It's an anti-psychotic.

I'm taken aback at the suggestion. But then I remember a friend telling me how she had been prescribed the same medication after feeling anxious and she seemed perfectly together to me.

'You are not psychotic, but you have a psychotic-like strength to your thoughts. You are thinking clearly about everything but this health issue.'

Dr Goria goes on to explain the way the two medications

work on the brain. One cools the brain, the other increases the serotonin levels. I'm a little cautious about taking two medications but agree to try.

A few weeks later, the Ashes series is in full swing in England and I'm back in Dr Best's office.

'How about those Aussies, I think they're really struggling against the swinging ball.'

We talk about Australia's opening batsman, Chris Rogers, and how he has made the most of his late opportunity in Test cricket. Why Steve Smith batted so well at Lord's to score a double century, but when the ball started to move in the air and off the wicket, he was less at ease (a weakness he corrected in the 2019 Ashes when he scored 671 runs at an average of 134).

Smith was the ever-obsessive, ever-moving Australian captain. Worse than Rafael Nadal on the tennis court. My mind is doing the sort of exaggerated fidgeting these players do before facing each ball.

'Ok, how are the latest medications going?' Dr Best asks.

I tell him that the pills made me feel calmer. For the first time for months I slept without waking in the middle of the night. How for a few days I felt euphoric and thought we had found the solution. It looked like a breakthrough. But then gradually, the more I took the dual medications, the more disconnected I felt. Like my mind was reaching every time I needed to complete a complex task.

I've also read the gunman who caused the Lindt Cafe siege and killed two people was on the same anti-psychotic.

'I want to go off them,' I tell him.

Dr Best has a resigned look on his face.

Tomorrow is another day.

But we're not there yet. Not even close. Breakfast time with four young kids is a constant uproar. It seems to me that all they do is scream, cry, argue and often don't pay attention to anything we tell them. Anxiety intensifies the sharpness of sound. Like it's blaring out of the speaker right next to my head. Around them, I'm more irritable by the moment.

The noise sets off the cockatiel that sets off the dogs that sets off me or Ann calling out to the dogs to be quiet. That sets off the kids.

Our house has also become the neighbourhood drop-off zone for other kids.

The parents, I'm sure, don't realise the extra strain another child places on an already noisy and disrupted house. More kids means more noise. More pointless arguments. The way they yell out of excitement. The endless questions and attention seeking.

'Dad, where are you?'

'Dad, what are you doing?'

'Dad, can you help me fix this?'

They wear me down. The cockatiel's screech wears me down even more. This same caged bird that makes a sound like a landline telephone. Jack is his name. He was supposed to be staying for just a little while. When the owner, Ann's mother, who'd come down to stay for a week, left with the bird, two-year old Harry had tears running down his face.

'Jack stay,' he kept repeating.

And so Harry's grandmother went home, but Jack remained.

Some days when the kids were at school, I'd sit down in the study to do some work. Jack would make a sound like the telephone. I'd make my way down the hallway to the phone.

Jack would stop ringing when I neared his cage.

'You little bastard.'

He'd also kick the seed onto the floor. As I'd sweep it up, Jack would start up, chirping away like he was instructing me.

'There you go, Jack,' I'd say before putting the dustpan and broom away.

And then he'd look me square in the eye and kick more seed out of the cage.

One morning I snap. Not at Jack, but at my eight-year-old son Ambrose who at times can be more than rambunctious. This morning he's in my face trying to make a joke.

'Stop that please, Ambrose.'

He ignores me.

'Stop that please.'

My voice is getting louder. He doesn't stop.

Then I push him away and yell at him, 'Just stop it!'

Immediately I can see the shock and hurt in his face.

I say I'm sorry and a few minutes later Ann loads the kids into the car for school. Ambrose refuses to look at me.

I ring work to tell them I need to take the day off. I don't tell them what has happened or how I am feeling.

I go into the shed and stand on a chair. Look at the ceiling to see if there are rafters I could tie a piece of rope to. Imagining just getting it finished. I know that Ann is out for the morning.

Other days I try holding my breath under water in the pool to simulate what it might feel like drowning. I've thought about jumping off the Busselton Jetty and floating out to sea. Into oblivion. Into a world of silence, without the thoughts.

But today is different. There is an urgency to how I feel. I walk to the car and start driving to Bunnings to buy the rope.

As I drive, my mind returns to a conversation with Dr Goria.

'How dark have these thoughts become?'

When I tell him just how dark, he said, 'There's no coming back, Barry. You must realise that. There is no coming back, Barry.'

He placed an emphasis on my name each time he said it. He looked at me and talked slowly. 'It would also cause devastation for your family for the rest of their lives.'

I do a U-turn and drive to the beach. It's winter, but I know the value of cold water on my body. I don't have a towel or bathers with me so I walk into the ocean in my undies. I don't give a fuck about what anyone thinks, not that there are many others around, just the regular Indian lady and a bloke in his sixties with a long grey beard.

Seaweed fills the shallow waters. I slowly walk into the ocean. To waist-height. Then I plunge and then plunge again into the cold waters of Busselton. I gasp as I rise to the surface and I realise I'm alive. My mind is clearer. I lift my arms in triumph.

The biting breeze accentuates the chill of the ocean as I watch the waves roll in. Soon the warmth of the car is welcoming, and I wonder what I was thinking earlier in the day. Tears come easily.

On the way home guilt washes over me.

The way I spoke to Ambrose. The time I have wasted. The effect of my illness on my family. The pleasures I am missing out on.

I drop into the newsagent and buy some of Ambrose's favourite footy cards and take them to his school. I ask for him at the office. He looks a little uncertain. We sit on a bench next to the school courtyard.

'I'm sorry for yelling at you today.'

He looks down at the ground and smiles. An embarrassed smile.

I hand him the footy cards which he checks while we talk. He looks at me and holds up one of the cards, a special one, one that has a three-dimensional element to it. We say goodbye. I kiss him on the head and he jogs back to his classroom, looking down at his footy cards as he goes. I drive to the ocean and look out. I always seem to end up here when I feel I have nowhere else to turn.

When the fuck is this going to end?

Tomorrow is another day.

You don't notice how thick congealed blood is until you've wiped it off white bathroom tiles.

Kylie Minogue's song 'I Should Be So Lucky' spins in my head. It's May 9, 1988, my twenty-fifth birthday. I'm due to catch up with an old friend for dinner. But the day was never going to end like that. After work I decided to drop into Mum's to see how Steve was going. I started the drive there then turned back. Then I changed my mind again and continued up Kensington Road, past my old school, past my old cricket club, making my way through the base of the foothills to Mum's house.

Just in case.

The days before had brought a sense of relief. Steve's behaviour had calmed. For the first time in years, he seemed content. The normality was in its own way disconcerting. The house was dark, the windows closed and there was an unsettling silence. Steve's car was in the drive.

I opened the unlocked door. A double cassette was on Mum's dining room table – Paul McCartney's *All the Best!*

'Steve, are you there?'

That's when I saw them: the bloodstained footprints tracking from the lounge to the bathroom. Then back to Steve's bedroom. The bath was caked in blood, like a thick soup.

I walked to his bedroom where I found him lying on his back. There was so much blood that at first I wondered if someone has broken in and stabbed him.

His wrists had been slit straight.

For a moment I considered walking out. To leave him to it in this bloody mess he's created. To leave him to die.

He'd once told me the movies always get it wrong when they show people who slash their wrists.

'The proper way to do it is straight down,' he said as he demonstrated, pretending to slice a knife across his wrist. 'For maximum effect.'

There were bloodied scissors on the floor.

Steve looked dead. His eyes were closed. He made no movement or sound. Then I saw that his diaphragm was slowly moving up and down. As I apply a towel to his wrist, he raised his head slightly just off the pillow.

'The blood's coagulated, I've stopped bleeding,' he said in a condescending whisper.

Once again, I phoned 000 and the ambulance crew took Steve out on a stretcher.

'Lucky you found him,' the medico said. 'It looks like he's lost an enormous amount of blood.'

After they'd gone, I rang Mum who'd gone to visit my brother Ralph in Canberra on her first holiday for years.

Dad comes to Mum's to help clean up. Father and son wipe the blood from the tiles and carpet for close to three hours. There is a deep silence as we mop.

Later we sit at an Italian restaurant on the edge of the city. I don't feel much like eating.

14. Waxing and waning · 1988–91/2015–16

Steve's mental health goes from highs to lows. When he's doing ok, he doesn't like the lack of libido and other side effects that come with the medication cycle. Steve attracts a raft of girlfriends, from the physio to the nurse to the occupational therapist. Steve knows how to give compliments and when he splits up with one girl he returns to the Beaumont church to meet another.

Steve settles for a while then marries his girlfriend Kathy. We all celebrate their union in high style at a reception in the South Terrace Gardens. I am the best man while Andy from the Christmas Day disappearance a few years back is another of the groomsmen. Dad gives a speech about the origin of the word honeymoon while Mum helps entertain the guests.

But then things deteriorate when real life hits.

Steve quits his job as a physio, starts various courses and fails to finish any of them. He is in and out of hospital. He believes he is being poisoned by his surroundings and refuses to visit my parents' houses, although they often spend time tidying up his new home in Mt Barker.

One time, Steve is hospitalised for three months and no one visits him. He develops septicemia and almost dies. We've all reached our limit trying to cope with the overflow of anxiety his actions have brought. A constant nervousness follows me around. After years of waiting for the next disaster, I'm sure it is just around the corner. Like a leg spinner to a batsman in full flight on an oval with short square boundaries. Just waiting to be hit for another six.

Shane Warne initially looks like a bogan gifted a baggy green. A disastrous Test debut against India at the SCG in 1992 proved the sceptics right. Bowling against Indian batting giants Shastri, Vengsarkar, Azharuddin, Tendulkar and Kapil Dev, Warne is hit around the SCG for 150 off 45 overs. He barely looks like taking a wicket, although he eventually does.

Terry Jenner, the former Aussie leggie and Warne's mentor, knows a bit about life as well. He hadn't long come out of eighteen months behind bars after he stole money to feed a gambling addiction. His former skipper Ian Chappell helped Jenner back into the cricket community, immediately removing any possibility of him being shunned for having served time.

Jenner knows the sound of the fizz of a leggie who could rip the ball. He can also handle a rough diamond like Warne: 'You're fat, drink way too much beer and smoke like a chimney and have never had to sacrifice anything.'

Warne starts training and eating properly. He takes a match-winning five-wicket haul against the West Indies at the MCG and then turns a Test match with a vital breakthrough against Sri Lanka.

Then in a single moment, Warne shakes the cricketing world when he dislodges Mike Gatting's off-bail at Manchester, in the First Test in 1993.

The plan was hatched seven days before when Warne

was smashed around the picturesque Worcester ground by Graeme Hick. But that was smoke and mirrors. This is the new-look, Test-match Warne – trim, short bleached hair, white zinc on his nose and lips, a XXXX advert on his shirt and, as we will soon discover, he can do anything with a cricket ball in his hand.

The camera is distant, then closes in. Just a couple of steps run-up, the delivery floats to the leg side and then swerves back, bounces, and breaks from outside leg stump to hit the top of off stump. Warne pumps the air while his team mates surround him in celebration.

Richie Benaud: 'He's done it ... he's started off with the most beautiful delivery.'

Gatting looks down the pitch spellbound. The groan of the England dressing room can almost be heard in Australia, where I am lying on the couch at Mum's.

A leg-spinning revolution that will last two decades has arrived.

I seek solace in nature's gifts – like a crisp spring morning at the beach.

It's December 2015 and a ninety-nine-year-old man works in a Busselton newsagent. I wonder how he does it. Not just the working but also the living. One sustains the other. He's there for half a day, seven days a week, from dawn.

I think of him as I adjust my eyes to the light like Ian Chappell when he walked out to bat. I walk up the driveway past the silence of the children's bedrooms to the garage. Reverse the car and turn the radio on to hear the local news. The companionship is more important than ever as it briefly helps me get out of my own head. I'm still searching for a resolution. An exit from the anxiety. I'm drawn again to the ocean like a magnetic force.

As I drive through the near-silent streets of town at sunrise, there's a freshness to the day. The newsagent in the main street has its lights on. The old man must be in there stacking the papers for the day. I pull into the ocean-front car park, next to a vista of lawn tennis courts. Council workers have made an early start.

A leaf blower interrupts an otherwise tranquil scene of early morning walkers and joggers. Swimmers glide through the smooth waters. I stroll the boardwalk fifty or so metres beyond the temporary beach volleyball courts. The remnants of bird shit that litter its surface crumble beneath my feet.

I plunge into the ocean and the coldness bites. Come up for air and lie on my back, allowing the buoyancy of the water to hold me. Duck dive like a kid and resurface, and take a few deep breaths. The jetty railing is slippery as I haul myself out.

An uplifting feeling before work is all I hope for. Moments of pleasure, not a continual stream of feeling. Not yet. I drive past the newsagent on the way back and see the old man standing at the door talking to a customer.

A new day has begun, and my nerves start to jangle again.

Steve's playing with his beard and telling me how ECT fried his brain. He's twisting it like he's trying to solve a problem, telling me how the nurses were lining him up. Putting nodes on his head. They were ready to charge but something went wrong.

'This guy's in trouble.'

That's what one of the nurses said. Like *One Flew over the Cuckoo's Nest*. But I'm not sure how reliable a narrator Steve is.

I'm asking Dr Best about ECT. I want to be jolted back to when I felt well.

'Do I need it?'

There's a slight pause and then he laughs but not in a mocking or patronising way. 'It might work for some, but I don't think we quite need to go down that path. We'll keep working with Dr Goria. He knows what he's doing.'

Exhaustion is my companion. For six weeks I stay in rental accommodation in Bunbury on weekdays to save the daily commute. I'm like a drive-in drive-out worker as every bit of energy is sucked out of me.

'You sound tired.' It's my old friend Mark who's called to say hello.

I'm walking along the foreshore of Back Beach in Bunbury seeking a boost. It makes no difference. I'm also trying to write another book in the middle of this whirlwind. It's about the 1977 Centenary Test, the one I was obsessed with all those years ago.

The words don't come easily.

As well as the full-time work.

And trying to help raise four kids, although I'm not much help.

There are deadlines everywhere.

Mark says, 'Just tell the publisher you won't have it ready.'

'I'll just keep working through it.'

I don't want to let anyone down. Not Ann and the kids, not the ABC, not my publishers and not my friends.

By February 2016, I know I'm fucked. Fucked in that way when you're juggling balls and you know you've thrown one too high. Fucked in the way I felt when my bike flipped a complete

360 when I was twelve, riding down steps at Ridge Park near where Dad lived. I didn't tell Mum and Dad about that. Just like I don't tell them much about how I'm feeling.

'Just some anxiety,' I say to them when they call. 'I'm ok, just struggling a little bit.'

I spend part of my lunchtime at work escaping the office and lie on a park bench trying a mindfulness exercise. I'd been to see a psychologist, more at Ann's urging than anything. He was a kindly middle-aged man who had worked with refugees on Christmas Island and who walked me through a meditative scenario. But nothing sticks.

'This will take time. You need to persevere.'

I'm still too wired to get into any state close to mindfulness, whatever that is.

We do a practice.

'Imagine yourself in a place that you associate with relaxing, like an isolated beach on a summer's day. Now take a few deep breaths.'

I close my eyes and try to take in the sound of the waves rolling onto the shore. The seagulls squawking. Picture the towel I'm lying on. The book I have with me.

'You'll need to rehearse this every day. Just a few minutes a day to begin with.'

That's why I'm lying on a park bench in Bunbury, under a palm tree. But I can't get past the laying my towel down on the sand as invasive thoughts return.

I sit up. Take a few deep breaths and decide to head back.

I ring Dr Best.

'Are you ok?'

'I've never felt this bad.'

'It's ok,' he reassures me, 'if you feel like things are becoming too much, take half a lorazepam.'

I keep a spare in my wallet for emergencies and most days I wonder at what point of the day I'll need to take it.

I try to hold off for as long as possible.

'Call me after work and let's talk some more.'

I drop the pill on my tongue and immediately start to feel better. I feel it slowly disintegrating and my thoughts stop racing. I notice what a beautiful day it is.

The Indian Ocean comes into focus and I start to feel like I did when I was well.

It only lasts a little while and by the time my radio show starts it's beginning to wear off. The anxiety returns, more relentless than ever.

I get through the three hours feeling distracted and distant.

I walk in the dark to my car, listening to waves crashing onto the rocks near the shore as rain lightly falls. I start to drive home and then stop.

I call Dr Best and tell him I think I need to be in hospital.

'You will feel better at home,' he tells me.

We talk for a while and in the end, I agree.

'I'll speak with Dr Goria in the morning. I'll give you a call after that.'

15. Defeating the West Indies · 1995–2000/2016

The Caribbean is full of small grounds, lightning outfields and slow pitches. There are early injuries to Australian fast bowlers.

The West Indies have been undefeated for fifteen years (at home they conquer all for twenty-two). Playing them is like climbing Mt Everest without oxygen. The big blond Queenslander Carl Rackemann flies in to bolster reserves and even has to borrow an Australian blazer. There's a carnival atmosphere: bands play music and a smell of ganja floats across the ground. David Hookes and Geoff Boycott commentate while Michael Holding (the lethal bowler once known as 'Whispering Death') carries out pitch reports on pay TV. Cable & Wireless adverts are spread across the stumps.

Glenn McGrath emerges as a quality pace bowler as Australia wins in under three days at Barbados. There's rain at Antigua and a heavily grassed underprepared wicket at Trinidad. Steve Waugh takes on Curtly Ambrose, toe to toe with verbal slings, until the West Indian captain Richie Richardson intervenes. The moment is splashed across front pages around the world.

Then at Kingston, Jamaica, it turns. Mark Waugh adds another stick figure to his thigh pad, scoring his eighth Test match century. His twin Steve is dropped by Courtney Brown in his 40s, then scores a double century.

The West Indies batsmen fall to the spell of Paul Reiffel, Brendon Julian and Shane Warne. When Kenny Benjamin edges Warne to Taylor, it's all over.

Back in the dressing room, recently retired Allan Border enthusiastically claps his hands.

It's Australia's first series win against the West Indies since 1975/76. Border, throughout his fifteen-year Test career, was never able to do it. David Boon, replete with droopy moustache, pulls the top off a beer in the alcohol-soaked change room.

'I've been waiting ten years for this,' he says.

We all have.

When the World Wide Web arrives, barely anyone notices.

I watch on as the cursor on Dad's 386 computer blinks.

'You need to be patient, it takes a while to power up.'

Dad is in his late sixties, sitting in a pair of shorts and the old collared shirt he uses for gardening. White socks and sandals. He's got a bandaid on his knee that he must have knocked somehow. He reaches to the back of the computer and attaches a phone line to the wall before switching on a small modem. Lights flash and the phone dials and there's a screeching noise as modems connect across the ether.

Dad's way of communicating is by telling stories or showing me how to do things. Sometimes when he talks, he just starts mid-sentence.

'The World Wide Web,' he says. 'It's basically computers linked via big servers around the world.'

He'd used a version of it for years at work. His whole life was about computers, back when huge mainframe computers filled an entire room.

'There's Internet Relay Chat, that's all about cricket. People chat to each other on IRC in real time.'

We find scorecards of old Test matches.

Dad shows me how to type the http://.

'Hypertext transfer protocol,' he explains.

Netscape's arrival signifies a quantum shift: a browser with a graphic interface.

There is no Google back then. We use AltaVista. Dad shows me Cricinfo, a website created by expatriate academics, providing up-to-date information about Test matches around the world and ball-by-ball commentary. There's an interactive section where you can upload articles. I write a book review for *Bradman: An Australian Hero* by the English Lord Charles Williams and write to Sir Donald telling him about it.

He replies a few days later, on New Year's Eve, 1996.

'There's a website called Bradman which has attracted an astonishing six thousand hits,' he writes.

I don't know it yet, but I've found a path to the future.

It took Mum a while after her relationship with Larry to trust men again but she eventually meets Ron, a former accountant, who starts coming over to tea once a week so they can have a meal and then watch a movie together.

His calm nature is good for her. He provides some moral support and distracts Mum if she starts to complain about Dad. She laughs more around Ron and seems less worried about things.

Eventually they go together to the United States and travel the west coast on a bus tour, taking in San Francisco, the Grand Canyon and later Disneyland.

Ron is a gentle soul who loves cricket and its writings. We

bond over old-time writers like Neville Cardus, Ray Robinson and Jack Fingleton. We talk about titles like *Days in the Sun*, *Between Wickets* and *Brightly Fades the Don* as Mum looks on slightly bewildered.

He's even got Clarrie Grimmett's 1932 book *Tricking the Batsman*.

I tell him how Clarrie presented the book to Dad at Cowandilla Primary after he topped the bowling averages. How Clarrie rode to the school on his bike, although Dad forgot to ask the 'Fox' to sign his book.

Ron loves that story.

Anxiety comes and goes. Sometimes it stays too long, normally near the end of the school term when occasionally I have to take a mental health day.

The hardest part is ringing the deputy principal, who has an acerbic tongue and a sharp sense of humour. She's academically progressive, urging a more inclusive approach to teaching Aboriginal history. Her first husband died in a plane crash, but it's rarely ever mentioned. Not beyond whispers on yard duty away from the staffroom. Some days, grief seems to hang over her like a cloud, while her faith provides a buoyancy.

I dial the touchpad next to the answering machine on a small table that flashes with messages. Then stop and start again.

She always picks up after two rings, no matter the hour you call.

'Feeling a bit crook, sorry I won't be in today.

'Ok Barry, I hope you feel better soon.'

My mind relaxes but I feel a pang of guilt. My mission for the day though is clear: head to the beach to clear the mind. I walk the upstairs concrete path that runs beside flats, moving quickly so I don't catch the eye of my neighbours.

Reach the car and reverse my orange Volkswagen.

It takes two goes so I don't hit the iron fence behind. Ease out to Wakefield Street onto Dequetteville Terrace, past Prince Alfred College's main oval, and what used to be the straight of the Adelaide Street Circuit for the Australian Grand Prix.

The VW with its dodgy muffler rumbles as I pick up speed and move down North Terrace. It briefly feels like the start of the school holidays. Slowing down in the city traffic, I watch the hustle and bustle of the suits going to work. Then down to West Beach to feel the ocean breeze and to take a swim and feel the sand under my feet.

On the way back, I drop into a pawnshop.

'How can I help, mate?' asks the bloke with matted hair and yellow nicotine nails.

'I'm ok, just looking.'

'What are you looking for?'

I think: Some peace of mind.

The CD racks swell with unwanted memories. The shop, I'm certain, has no soul.

I wonder about the circumstances of their sale. A CD has a photo of Jimmy Barnes after a big night out lying in a bath with a headband on. *East*. A 1980 release that spent almost two years on the charts. Japanese writing melts across Barnes' headband while a white sheet full of newspapers and books surrounds him.

'That'll be five dollars mate.'

Drive past the old Keswick railway station where my grandfather Cecil used to work.

'Ride your bike up to Keswick, Les, the Yanks are here.'

Dad chatted to the US soldiers as they handed out gifts, like perfume to young women and chocolates to the kids.

The Yanks.

'Oversexed, overpaid and over here.'

They looked smart in their uniform.

I wind down the window and feel the breeze on my face. My head feels lighter. I've gotten over the hump of anxiety. For now.

Twenty years later, I'm sitting in a park in Margaret River. Crying.

It's the day after the psychologist gave me a questionnaire. The one I had trouble filling in. The one that revealed I hated myself. That I was full of self-loathing.

That day I'd been to the gym, been for a swim, driven to Margaret River. Even gone to my favourite bookstore. Nothing worked. Not a fucking thing.

I've reached the end of my tether when Dr Best rings.

'The psychologist said you weren't travelling so well. Where are you now?'

I tell him how I've managed to get through the worst part of the day and am about to go and have lunch at a pub.

'If you want a spell, I can get you into a clinic in Perth.' He sounds more worried than before.

'I'm ok.'

'You don't sound ok. There is a room available. I can get you in.'

'I think I'm over the worst of today. It's ok.'

'I'll call you later today to see how you are going. If you feel like you need to talk, call me.'

That's when I head to the small park at the end of the main street of Margaret River, where it all becomes too much. I'm broken. I'm riding the medication wave, but I keep getting tipped off. I get through the day.

Tomorrow is another day.

'Hey Barry, well done, your name is in this cricket book.'

My friend Chris is holding *Cricket's Hall of Shame*, the one with the streaker on the cover flashing at the umpire. Dave Warner's latest. Warner the musician and author. Not Warner the Australian ultra-aggressive opening batsman whose reputation was tarnished by the ball-tampering scandal in South Africa. The one deemed by the public and the press to be the mastermind.

'Have a look Barry, they've given you an acknowledgement in the foreword of the book.'

Chris is smiling.

I'd written a brief piece for Cricinfo about the life and murder of former New South Wales player and Test aspirant Claude Tozer who'd been shot dead by his mistress in the 1920s.

It was the first time I'd seen my name in hardcopy as a writer. July 1998.

Chris was one of life's encouragers. We'd first met at a sports history group full of mainly middle-aged blokes. He was a psychologist and a lover of cricket's esoteric events.

Chris and I spoke the same language and used it to describe life's ups and downs. If you were 'batting on a wet wicket', you were struggling. 'Bowling one short of a length' was to make a provocative statement. 'Treading on all three stumps' was an act of self-sabotage; 'refusing to walk off when your stumps were shattered' was ignoring the signs life was sending you.

For a while there, Chris seemed to disappear and didn't answer my calls.

Then someone told me. Chris had lost his job, his house and almost everything. He was saddled with enormous debt. He was ill and in hospital. A month or so later when he was out, a friend provided a spare room free of charge while he got back on his feet.

Chris spends his days at cafes, treating them like an office, slowly rebuilding his mind and sense of self. He meets various friends to share news from the daily newspapers.

He tells me he's lost some mates because of the stigma of his illness.

'Not the sorts of friends I'd want to keep.'

We met every week for about twelve months to talk about my journalism studies. He'd offer ideas about the Sturt book I was writing, and later became a guest on my community radio sports show.

We were like a good opening batting combination, encouraging each other with every milestone passed.

Chris re-established himself as a leading psychologist and mainstream media commentator. We'd joke about his comeback.

'What a second innings. What will be the title of your book?' I'd ask.

'From the Adelaide Clinic to the Adelaide Club,' he would reply with his booming laugh.

When I am in the turmoil of 2014 to 2016, I occasionally ring Chris for advice, not as a psychologist but as a friend.

The topic of medication comes up. I've got to the point where I am getting sick of trying. Sick of their failure to have any effect. Sick of the way taking them makes me feel, especially early on when they can worsen anxiety and depression.

His advice is succinct. He listens to everything I say and once he is sure I've finished he says, 'Sometimes you need help to get out of a hole.'

He is right.

I am in a hole and I can't get out on my own.

Interior light reflects off the wood panelling. Elevated desks in the courtroom stand out in the solemn, ritualistic and ceremonial environment.

I walk to the court via the multilayered marble staircase in the Sir Samuel Way Building in Adelaide's centre next to the Central Market.

A few weeks earlier the letter arrived, and I collected it from the row of letterboxes strewn with junk mail.

It was from the sheriff's office and, at first, I thought it was a joke.

I walked by the lawn that ran alongside the downstairs flats, reading the letter. I am just past the first paragraph when –

'Oh, hmm, he's cute.'

It was one of the drag queens who lives upstairs. There were two of them on the balcony dressed up for a night out. I'd met them a few nights earlier when I knocked on their door to ask them to turn the music down.

A young man wearing a baseball cap back-to-front had answered the door and stared back at me. Then one of drag queens came forward.

'Sorry, love, why don't you join us?'

I thought she was an attractive-looking girl, but I was too tired to accept the invite. The next day I saw them in daylight and it was clear they weren't women, well, not like the women I knew.

I kept reading the letter. I'd been called up for jury duty.

Strangely, the call to jury duty becomes the catalyst for resignation. I am bored with teaching. I recall Dad's words of him wanting 'to do', not teach, all those years before. I wanted to test myself beyond the safe environment of a private school in the eastern suburbs of Adelaide.

I resign from teaching at the Jesuit school I've been at for thirteen years. The J's as we called them. Those with a reputation for intellectual rigour, of far-ranging and free-thinking minds and an air of superiority.

The headmaster reads the letter with a wry smile. I'm not Catholic and I don't think he minds me going. I've always had the sense I am not quite religious enough for the J's.

By Boxing Day I'm in regional Victoria looking at the statue of Johnny Mullagh, the all-rounder who led the 1868 Aboriginal cricket tour of England. I'm soon driving to Melbourne to watch Australia play India at the MCG. It's a vast crowd. Indian expats raise the nation's blue flags around the outer. I travel back along the Great Ocean Road. The new millennium starts with a party, but I have an aching desire to sleep. The concern about the Y2K bug recedes in the early hours of the first day of the new year.

School holidays normally bring relief. Six weeks of sleeping in, watching cricket, reading, listening to music and writing. This year's different. I'm unemployed. There's uncertainty but also excitement. The two weeks leading into Christmas are spent twilight swimming in baking temperatures on the white sands of Aldinga Beach, forty-five minutes south of Adelaide, with a friend called Jane. She's just out of a brief marriage to an architect. We share the shack and a need for change. Dad and Dorothy visit. We eat ham and salad rolls, observing cars parked on the beach and parents building sandcastles with their kids while the sea gently nudges the shore.

That night Jane and I drive to the city and gather with a bunch of others outside the offices of the *Advertiser* to buy the paper fresh off the press for offers of admission to the University of Adelaide. It's like waiting to go into bat.

A crowd of mainly school leavers gathers. Papers are loaded from trucks onto the ground.

Thud, thud, thud.

Nearby voices echo excited sentiments.

'I've just made it into medicine ... here it is, here's your name,' says a young woman.

I'm scanning the columns of student ID numbers. Maybe I've missed mine on the first sweep through.

I scan again. Then Jane starts looking.

'It must be here somewhere.'

I've missed out on both law and computing.

'Don't worry, there's second offers,' says Jane.

It feels like not making the Kensington side for the 1985/86 premiership.

The drive back to Aldinga is silent.

As dawn breaks I walk the beach for a few hours.

A quick swim and out. A cool change is in. The ocean is choppy.

'Good morning,' Jane says. 'I wondered where you'd gone.'

She's holding breakfast on a tray with cereal, toast and jam, and sits next to me on the shack's balcony.

I stare at the ocean, not really listening when she says, 'Why don't you try journalism? You love writing.'

'Look you might be in luck. We've just started a postgraduate course and there was a student in earlier today wanting to defer. You'll need to take your qualifications and CV to the registration desk.'

I'm welcomed into a second-floor office of the journalism department of the University of South Australia by Ian Richards, the head of the school. His desk is a mess of papers and books.

'Horizontal filing', as Dad says.

Dr Richards is one of those blokes you instantly take a liking to, full of good humour and smiles.

We talk about the Indian tour of Australia and how fast Australia's opening bowler Brett Lee is.

My enrolment papers are lost for a week but two weeks later the call comes in.

'Well done,' Richards says. 'You're in. Come and see me next week and we can go through your subject options for the first semester.'

Jane and I celebrate with a drink.

'I've got something for you,' she says. She hands over a photo from the stay at Aldinga. 'I thought you might like this.'

A distant figure wandering into the ocean, a trail of footprints following along the beach behind him. Like he's walking toward something but he's just not sure exactly what it is.

16. Welcome to the real world · 2016/2000

Fishermen hang lines over the side and gleeful children drag in wriggling catches off the Busselton Jetty.

The 2016 Big Bash final is on.

I want my old life back. The one where I don't overthink and just get on with things. Today it's the Perth Scorchers vs Sydney Sixers, which turns out to be a television ratings bonanza. It's school holidays and kids can't get enough of it.

Cricket commentary buzzes through the speakers of small radios.

It's a day where I don't know where else to go. I walk to escape my thoughts, but they keep following me. I've already completed a few laps of the nearby oval and now I'm at the jetty, stuck like a needle on vinyl that just won't jump onto the next song.

I walk the 1.84-kilometre jetty twice by the time I decide I need help. Dr Best picks up straight away.

'A good game – why aren't you watching it? Are you outside somewhere?'

'I'm just on the jetty.'

There is a pause in Dr Best's voice and then, 'The jetty. What are you doing down there? Are you ok?'

I laugh. 'Yeah I'm ok.'

'Are you sure?'

I don't tell him of recent mornings when I have found myself at the jetty at the crack of dawn wondering what it would be like to jump off and let the ocean take me out to sea.

The Big Bash final is coming to a dramatic ending.

'When are you next seeing Dr Goria?' Dr Best asks.

I look out to the still waters. 'Next week.'

'Don't be down on yourself, life is full of different cycles. This is just one period.'

I keep walking to the end of the jetty.

That's one of the points that Dr Best has continually emphasised.

That I am normal and just going through a rough patch. He isn't too fond of labels.

At Manuka Oval, excited commentators' voices describe the match's climax.

I should be at home watching, not wandering like a lost soul on the jetty.

As a thirty-eight-year-old, my stints at local newspapers and even one as a sports reporter at a commercial TV station in Mt Gambier made me realise I had plenty to learn. Even so, it felt at times less like I was being guided and more like I was just an extra, unpaid worker. I loved print but baulked at the more glamorous TV news. It wasn't me.

Radio though became the medium with the most appeal.

'Why don't you come along?'

Emma's a fellow journalism student. Slightly in-your-face bolshie with a healthy sense of cynicism and a willingness to call out bullshit. That's one reason we get along. Wednesday nights I go to her place for tea to compare notes on assignments.

We're sitting around her dining room table while one of her housemates plays computer games on the TV in his bedroom.

'Come where?

'To 5UV, the community radio station. I've been going there for a few weeks.'

My radio experiences are limited to listening to cricket on ABC radio, Bazz and Pilko with Peter Plus and SAFM's Grant Cameron and the morning crew talking about the surf.

I'm walking long North Terrace trying to ignore the early morning traffic. It's 2000, but I am wearing black pants and a black turtle neck skivvy, like a man in a 1960s Peter Stuyvesant advert. I am heading to a meeting with the 5UV program director, P.J. Rose.

The glass doors slide open and I'm asked by the receptionist to take a seat. An announcer sits in the studio as a producer makes phone calls. I'm ushered down the corridor into an office.

P.J.'s sitting at a desk with papers and cassette tapes piled up. In her mid-fifties, she keeps her frizzy white hair closely cropped and says the word 'cunt' as she finishes a phone call, while beckoning me to sit. Word is that she works as a dominatrix in her spare time. She's solidly built and, I will come to learn, is as generous of spirit as she is different to the sheltered world of teaching I had come from.

P.J.'s the one who listened to the demo tapes. She's the one who decides if you deserved a chance to host your own show. She welcomes me with a broad American accent.

'Welcome Baaary.' Like she's a referee announcing a boxing match. 'Take a seeat.'

We chat.

In that interview, I must say something strange.

'Are you bit weird, Baaary?'

I laugh. 'Maybe.'

'That's good,' she smiles. 'We only like weirdos here.'

5UV has more politics than Canberra but is more like a big dysfunctional family full of diversity. Almost all are volunteers. Younger students wander the corridors broadcasting specialist music shows. Attractive blondes beam with radiant smiles as they practise reading the news in spare studios. A volatile South American husband and wife duo present a show about Latin American dancing music.

The camp veteran Ewart is there no matter what time of day or night you drop in. He has curly grey hair and dozy blue eyes behind glasses he habitually takes off and cleans.

'Lean back when you have a guest in the studio. Give them the chance to talk. It signals that you have confidence in them.'

One day he turns up with shiners under his eyes.

'I guess they didn't like poofs,' he says as he wanders past.

Diminutive Suzanne stalks the corridors with a stooped gait and a grim demeanor. She is a former BBC book critic in her seventies who spends every day pissed off, replying to gentle enquiries in a bitter tone. Her reviews are masterful. Every word counts. Other elderly people produce and present their own radio shows for Radio for The Third Age.

The buzz from being 'on air' is the closest excitement I had to playing cricket. That thrill of reading my first news bulletin reminds me of opening the batting and walking the mental tight rope knowing you could make a fool of yourself at any moment.

Seagulls drift away, squawking as they take off. The players leave the field for tea, and in the press box at Adelaide Oval reporters stand and stretch as they talk amongst themselves. I am in my second year studying journalism. I sit at the back of the room in no official capacity but I write match reports for practice.

The day before, former England captain and Channel Nine commentator Tony Greig emailed me about my request to interview him for 5UV.

Greig is the ultra-competitive, charismatic and extroverted South African who helped shepherd Kerry Packer's World Series cricket into existence and paid the price of losing the England captaincy.

'Thanks for the note, Barry, I can do a ten-minute interview for one hundred dollars.'

In my memory, I am taken back more than twenty years to when I'd watched Greig walk out to bat, swinging his arms in large circles on the second morning of the Centenary Test.

But now I don't have enough money to pay for an interview. The groceries win out instead.

A few weeks after that email exchange, I bump into Greig in the lift at the Adelaide Oval media centre. He's wearing the broad-brimmed hat he wears for his pitch reports.

It's just Tony and me in the lift. He walks in and stands in front of me and then looks up at the floor levels the way everyone does. At six foot seven he doesn't have far to look.

He pushes the button to take us downstairs.

'Well, how about that. I became the captain of England, well how about that.'

He isn't speaking to me, just mumbling under his breath. Perhaps he thinks I don't recognise him.

That summer in the media centre I watch Bill Lawry jump behind the lunch counter and help give out sandwiches, pies, pasties and cakes.

'Come and get it,' he hollers.

'Are you sure you don't want more?' he asks with a huge smile.

Not all are as friendly.

Peter Roebuck – who writes the foreword to David Frith's *Silence of the Heart* about cricketers who suicided, and who will eventually take his own life – once chastised me as we gathered during a rain break in play.

'Who sang the song "MacArthur Park"?' he enquired.

'Richard Harris first sang it, I'm pretty sure,' I said.

'Don't be so stupid,' he said as he reeled back in his chair.

The message from Roebuck is clear without him having to say anything.

'You're a nobody so shut up.'

Another day I struggle to open the press box door on the way out. Roebuck leans over me, clearing the way, but not before giving me a contemptuous look.

Not that he is all bad. Roebuck, to me, is one of those cricket-writing gods, blessed in a way that the rest of us could only dream about.

He once replies to my letter asking about his opinion on the role of public-school cricket in England's county and Test set-up. His response is prompt, succinct and helpful.

Roebuck's life was in many ways brilliant, yet deeply flawed. I still miss his commentary.

Red dirt provides an intoxicating backdrop to an azure sky. A smiling air hostess farewells passengers who walk gingerly down the small steps onto the tarmac. A strong breeze has me instinctively grabbing for the light metal rail. It feels like I've just opened a hot oven door, thirty-seven degrees in the shade.

I'm an Adelaide boy, more familiar with a gentle easing into warmer weather, walking the green lawns of the city's parklands still moist on spring nights, at least until October.

Alice Springs is the closest Australian town to any beach in the country – or the furthest away; it depends how you look at it.

That is the key to thriving in the Alice – the way that you look at it.

In the glaring light, squinting becomes second nature. It is a Sunday in early September and I'm about to go and work for Rupert Murdoch. The closest I will get to any connection with him is patting the head of Rupert, a dog of one of the main reporters.

My new workplace, the *Centralian Advocate*, is a bi-weekly tabloid bought by News Limited when the joint defence military facility (Pine Gap) was built just out of Alice Springs. It's housed in a one-level building on Gap Road that leads to the centre of town, and it accommodates journalists and subeditors as well as advertising and marketing departments.

The Goss Community Press fires up twice a week out the back.

Marilyn works the front office.

'Take a seat,' she says with a 'don't-fuck-with-me' look.

There's not much to see, just a few copies of the paper's recent edition. It's published every Tuesday and Friday.

'Mark will be with you shortly.'

Mark is probably in his late thirties, it's a bit hard to tell. He's bald with a red beard and a face that looks like it has half an eye on making mischief.

When he talks it sounds like he's speaking through gravel. One word rolls into another. It's only when he's stopped speaking you can work out what he was saying. But there is never any doubt what he means.

Mark was the first to interview the English backpacker Joanne Lees, after Bradley Murdoch tied her up and murdered her boyfriend Peter Falconio, on an outback stretch of road north of Alice Springs.

He is a legend in these parts.

The food van rolls by every morning at 11am for those who didn't pack lunch or don't give a fuck about their diet. The van's full of fried food, pastries, sweets and soft drinks.

I'll soon be a regular with Steve, the diabetic white-bearded features reporter, and Sharon, a marketing assistant with a keen ear for a dirty joke. I love the hustle and bustle of a newspaper office, the constant chatter of journalists working the phones.

The sports editor throws me some horseracing leads and contacts for me to chase as the first day passes in a blur. By the time I leave the sun is setting. I walk up Gap Road toward town and stop at the backpackers'-cum-nightclub called Melanka's. As people in their twenties mill about tables in various states of sobriety I order a lasagna and beer.

The crowd looks enthused, like they are just starting.

Career-wise I feel like I've just pushed a ball behind square leg and get off the mark.

Feedback from subeditors is brutal at times.

Kevin is a rotund man with the unnerving habit of laughing aloud while checking your copy.

'Which fucking idiot spelt fazed as phased?'

We all sink further into our chairs.

'Oh, it's you, Nicholls.' He turns around and looks down the rim of his glasses as if he's cleaning dog shit off his shoes. 'Fazed is the correct usage. F-A-Z-E-D,' Kevin says, standing and delivering.

He often leans back in his chair waiting for me to look up.

Some days he catches my eye and speaks about his glory days working as a London correspondent for Fairfax. When the industry was awash with commercial success, the rivers of gold in the form of classified advertisements bankrolled a large staff and generous conditions. Not that the work was easy, the journalists were often filing several times a day.

At those times, his eyes sparkle as they do when he describes his camping trips in the central desert on clear nights.

Other days Kevin wants to share his misery.

'Look around this office, Bazza. C'mon, look around.'

'Yes Kevin.'

He whispers in a conspiratorial tone. 'Not one person here is going to go onto anything better. Not one.' Then he smirks and turns to his desk, sighing loudly like all of this is beneath him.

Some are encouraging, like Glenn, the paper's main reporter, a part-time musician with a friendly nature. He does the odd singing gig to bolster his income, earning more from two days of crooning than he makes working at the paper.

The 2001 Falconio case hovers over the office like a ghost. One frantic afternoon, Glenn and a photographer are sent to Marla in South Australia, 400 kilometres south of Alice, where it's believed body parts have been found next to a dam.

All they find is a kangaroo's scrotum, causing loud laughter when the news is phoned through. A small two-par story is included on page ten.

The office is austere. Only one – shared – computer has internet access.

Media rivals call the paper *The Aggravate* because of its hard-nosed approach and often sensationalist headlines. Despite the lack of resourcing, it often sets the news agenda in the town. The paper rolls off the presses every Tuesday and Friday in the middle of the night. Workers are paid a pittance to insert advertising supplements.

'Ka-ching' is what the editor Jason says to lure journalists to accept a night shift of inserting. I can never bring myself to do it, but some are so desperate they haul themselves out of bed at ungodly hours to perform the task.

The Advocate is the first or last resort of journalistic desperadoes. Jason can smell a journalist's hunger for a story a mile off. He treats people with respect and rewards hard work.

One day he calls me into his office.

'Mate, I don't even understand this word you've used, serendipity,' he says, holding my copy with the tips of his fingers. 'So, the readers sure as hell won't. Write to a level a twelve-year-old could understand.'

When I make mistakes, he quietly takes me aside and shows me how to better report a story.

'You're overwriting. Look, we can get easily get rid of these words.'

Jason sends me to the Top End for a few days for the NTFL grand final, as a reward for the long hours I've been putting in. The steamy Darwin skies are a stark contrast to the desert heat of Central Australia. Ron Barassi stands next to the press box as giant insects fill the floodlit air. Barassi, the innovator who once shocked the football world by moving from the Melbourne Football Club to captain-coach Carlton, the first major tilt toward professionalism. Barassi, the premiership captain and firebrand coach in striped psychedelic shirts who bristled, inspired, ranted and raved at his teams.

I hustle up and tell him about a book I've written, about Sturt's 1978 SANFL one-point grand final loss to Norwood. The way it affected the club, like it did Collingwood after Barassi coached the Blues against them to an unlikely win, from 44 points behind in 1970.

He listens intently, smiling. 'I'll buy five copies.'

He writes me a cheque on the spot. I can't believe my luck.

I join the Memorial Club, just down the road from work. Sign in and show your membership card at the front. The 'no shoes, no service' policy is probably designed to keep Aboriginal people out.

The front bar of the club is full of blokes who cast wary glances at newcomers and swear like troopers. An ever-rotating cohort of backpacker barmaids serves up cold beer from a tap. The bar stinks with the smell of smoke while big screens broadcast Fox Sports.

On Thursdays, the Memo serves a special roast and smorgasbord for ten dollars. The line to enter is bigger than the one to get into the town's swimming pool on a forty-degree day.

The Memorial Club eventually goes into voluntary administration after the owners can't foot the ever-increasing insurance bill. It is being broken into on average three times a week.

Some days, with the heat, the isolation, the pressure of deadlines, living in a dingy flat, and with no close friends, I can feel myself tipping toward a mini depression.

The harshness of the town and its social problems are confronting at first. The cost of living in Alice Springs makes life difficult.

Land release is minimal with the government tied up in negotiations with native title holders. Houses and rentals are overpriced.

I'm not sure how long I'll be able to afford to work at the *Advocate*. That's what I tell the chief of staff one night over a beer.

I sometimes walk at the base of the MacDonnell Ranges, and I connect with the beauty of the country.

I come to believe the Aboriginal view is true. There is something special about the land and the feeling when you immerse yourself in it.

Walking it is replenishing, even though living in the Alice can be testing.

17. Things they don't tell you · 2016–17

Clouds carry loosely over a cool summer morning in Busselton. The smell of Trike's blanket hangs in the air. His collar sits behind me in the passenger seat as I travel in silence back from the vet. It's one of the things they don't tell you in the mental health manual. The stages when you feel so terrible that you missed things. Ann is doing her best to manage the kids but, in this maelstrom, our dog Trike is forgotten about. He is still fed, sheltered and walked but not looked after in the way he once was. He'd been blind for a few years and spent his days lying on the mat outside the back door or slowly negotiating his way around the various obstacles of a backyard.

We'd also bought a new kelpie called Frank who nipped at Trike's heels.

As the weeks of 2016 drag on for me, Trike's wanderings seem more aimless. Rather than walk along the pool fence and carefully feel his way past the kids' bikes and outside tables and chairs, he bumps into things.

'You'd better check on him,' says Ann. 'He's your dog.'

The last comment is more a reaction to her growing frustration with my illness. Like many partners of someone going through extended anxiety and depression, Ann is confused, tired and probably terrified.

Trike is a brown cocker spaniel much like the one I had as a kid. We got him not long into our relationship when we were living in the Northern Territory and we found out Ann was pregnant with Jacy.

Getting Trike house-trained was difficult. One day he squatted to do a shit on the lounge-room floor in front of us as we watched TV. By the time I'd scrambled to stop him he'd done two more dumps, creating a perfect triangle. From then on, we referred to the area as the 'Bermuda Triangle'.

Trike loved to chase the cockatoos that pecked at the grass at the nearby Traeger Park, home to the town's footy matches featuring sides from outlying Aboriginal communities as well as town clubs. His ears bounced up and down as he darted around, chasing screeching birds as they took off.

Ten years later, in 2016, I want to be there the day the vet puts Trike down. I'd missed Snoopy's death thirty years before and the grief, in a small way, has stayed with me.

Frank, who's around nine months old, sits next to Trike, howling.

In the morning, Frank follows me to the side gate as I pick Trike up and carry him to the car.

The vet examines Trike's skinny frame and ragged teeth.

'This dog's teeth are terrible. He's got an infection. We could try antibiotics, but they might not work. He's a very sick dog.'

I feel ashamed. Shame is big when you are depressed. You feel shame about every mistake you believe you've made. I stroke Trike's head when the vet prepares the injection to put him to sleep.

'He'll be more comfortable this way,' the vet says. 'He'll take a couple of deep breaths before he passes.'

There is nothing and then he twice exhales deeply.

Soon his body is lifeless. Another link to a time when I was more present had been severed.

There is beauty in the moment, but it's been another terrible day.

The sound of kids splashing echoes around the indoor swimming pool, a heavy smell of chlorine fills the air and steam covers the windows. I'm watching Harry's school swimming classes and run into one of the other dads, a GP.

'Why aren't you at work?' It sounds abrupt, like he's making a judgement.

'A bit of long service,' I reply. It's a lie but I'm in no mood to tell him why I'm off work. I'd loaded up on two and a half lorazepam to get me through the day.

I wonder why he isn't at his workplace, but I don't ask.

When I get home, Dylan, my case coordinator, a gentle bloke who lines up appointments with Dr Goria, calls.

'I just thought I'd ring to say hello and see how you are going.'

We chat briefly then a few minutes later he calls back.

'Hey, do you mind if I drop something over to you?'

He's told me about this book called *The Happiness Trap: Stop Struggling, Start Living*.

'Don't worry I'm fine.'

Ann had earlier bundled the kids up and took them to see her parents in Perth on a planned visit. I stay in Busselton. Socialising has become too difficult for me.

There's a knock at the door and I walk past the family photos hung in the passageway. Dylan hands me the book and stays for just a few minutes to see I'm ok.

I wander to the Busselton foreshore as the afternoon

sunshine fades and a cool breeze sweeps through.

'Hey Barry, I thought that was you.' It's Dr Goria, who's also here to watch the sunset.

We shake hands.

'How are you going?' he asks.

I shrug. 'Slowly.'

We chat for a while then part ways. It is another small gesture that means a lot. I get the feeling that they're looking out for me.

'Don't wish your life away,' Mum used to say to me when I was a kid wanting to grow up quicker. Wanting the time to pass and counting down the days until the next milestone whether that was a birthday, Christmas or the next cricket match.

But that's what I've been doing. I wonder if I'll ever come back, like I used to after a bad run of outs when batting. I'd survive the first few overs, scratch around, and then middle one ball that would make its way to the boundary. Get into double figures and suddenly I'd be seeing the ball earlier and able to do what came naturally.

To watch the ball more carefully.

The ball comes into focus. I watch it all the way onto the bat, the same as Greg Chappell did all those years ago when he came back from his run of ducks.

A leap of faith is needed. It's the only way I am going to make some progress.

I'd previously taken annual and long service leave to try to cope but it hadn't made much difference.

Now I need to do everything I can to regain my sense of equilibrium. To get well again. It's taken me this long to realise that I need time off work. I needed to stop fighting against the anxiety, ruminations and depression. To stop trying so hard to get things right.

I clear all my items out of my desk. I'm the only one in the office. I've never felt so lonely. Like a boy in short pants on that first day of school at Linden Park Primary all those years ago. I slowly pack up and send emails explaining I need to take some time off.

I gather my personal items, like photos of Ann and the kids, and pack them into a box. I feel relief as I drive away, knowing the daily hour-and-a-half commute and slog through three hours of radio is behind me.

I believe that I'll never work again. At least not in radio where you need to be able to perform, but maybe that is the depression talking.

'I'm finished,' I say to Ann when I got home.

'No, you'll come back. You just need some time.'

The first few days of leave I don't know what to do but I soon settle into a routine. Once the kids have gone to school, I ride the kilometre or so down to a cafe in Busselton. Sunlight streams in as I drink coffee and read the newspapers, hoping my mind will slowly resurrect.

I'm reminded of my old friend Chris all those years ago. The way he would sit at Café Bravo on the Parade in Adelaide using research to help restore his sanity.

Some days I lie in my daughter Jacy's hammock outside our lounge room. I grab a blanket to warm myself, read and often just hope that I'll drift off to sleep while the world goes on around me.

Dr Goria's talking to me again about medications. Nothing's worked so far.

'Do you want to persist, or bring out the big guns? These are a much stronger drug... and you'll need to have an ECG to check your heart.' He's leaning forward, like he's reaching for a solution.

The drug he suggests is Clomipramine, more aimed at OCD. It comes in small doses, so you need to take a lot of it.

At first it doesn't feel much different. After a few weeks I go back to see him and report that there are no obvious side effects, which surprises even Dr Goria.

Then slowly, just slowly, the intensity of my thoughts reduces. It is like sitting in a speeding car that is gradually slowing down. Changing down the gears.

Some days are better than others. These days I feel happier, but at other times I feel as if I am carrying a dead weight on my back.

The trend though is toward improvement.

My perspective starts to return, and my mind stills.

I stop looking up information and start experiencing longer moments of pleasure. I buy some new clothes and get a haircut. Little things to show I am recovering. My appetite returns. I start reading more deeply again.

'We're finding the sweet spot.'

That's how Dr Goria describes it. He's using cricket's language again to describe how it feels to hit one in the middle. When the ball sails away from you to the boundary. Like a weight of responsibility is slowly sliding off my shoulders.

It's the first time I've felt this way for ages.

A few weeks later I return to work, on my fifty-third birthday.

Work colleagues greet me warmly, but I just want to get the day over and done with. When it comes to turn the microphone back on, I feel better. Gone is the anxiety.

I don't feel 100 percent, but I do feel infinitely better. As the weeks progress, I find a resolution to everything I have been worried about.

The cycle is broken.

Dr Best smiles as he asks. Just as he knows I was battling before, he knows I am on the way back.

'How are you feeling?'

'Much better.'

'You're looking good. I think we're getting somewhere. This is Dr Goria's good work.'

I can also laugh again. A bellyaching laugh that lifts the spirits.

Clear vision. The doubting and the humiliation are over, and my confidence is rebuilding.

Another innings has begun.

The hurricane of the previous twenty-four months has left, and I've been back at work full-time for two months. Now small doses of medication are gradually weaned to nothing.

My appointments with Dr Goria have ended.

I take a short holiday to Adelaide to see Mum and Dad. We're down at Brighton Beach having lunch when the song 'Smoke Gets in Your Eyes' plays in the background.

Dad's ears prick up and he again tells me the story of his family's connection with the song. Mum, whose hair has changed from grey to white, smiles and speaks of memories of their courting days.

'That's where your mum used to sit. Under the jetty.'

They are both gentler now. Dad's colouring at the edge of his light blue eyes has started to fade. Some of his intellectual energy has subsided. His mind is still sharp, especially when it comes to longer-term details.

Some good comes from the ageing process.

Mum drives her car to pick up Dad from his house once a fortnight.

'There's this nice elderly lady who comes around and picks me up every few weeks and we all go out to lunch with Steve and his family,' Dad tells me with a smile.

Mum has also mellowed. There is no lingering animosity.

'It's all a long time ago now, I've forgotten what all the arguing was about,' she says.

I meet Steve for coffee. His condition for years has stabilised, although he needs a carer. He is in some ways institutionalised in his own home. He hasn't worked for decades.

Steve is lucky to be alive. Many with his severity of illness no longer are. These days he goes to a men's group and is less agoraphobic.

Steve develops a love of writing and has a poem published. I wonder sometimes about what he could have achieved as a writer if he hadn't been so ill.

'Hey Barry, I went to the library the other day and asked about your books.'

It's his way of saying thank you.

The next week I'm back at work and grab a coffee at the van that operates on the Bunbury beachfront. Smooth water, calm thoughts.

I look at my phone. It's 9.33am. Gran is watching over me again.

I'm back.

I'm fucking back.

The smooth green oasis stretches on. We're looking out over the eighteenth hole as weary golfers walk the final distance with the clubhouse in sight. It's Dad's ninetieth birthday at the Mount Osmond Golf Course.

We sit at a long table. Mum's there, along with Ralph and Steve and their wives' kids and some grandkids. Talk turns to the Ash Wednesday bushfires of February 1983, that day of forty degrees and soul-destroying winds, when flames swept across two states killing seventy-five people. When more than 3,000 buildings smouldered in ruins.

I watched the flames burn along Hayward Drive wiping out parts of Themeda Reserve. The fire randomly took out houses at the edge of the golf course until moving beyond the Old Bullock Track and across Waterfall Gully Road. Then it tracked east to Mount Lofty destroying the look out and nearby houses. The top of Greenhill Road was obliterated and five people lost their lives on Yarrabee Road. Smoke hung over the city like a dust storm

I watched the fire scream up the hill near Dad's house as Australian Crawl's *Sons of Beaches* roared at full volume on my car cassette. Fire trucks cleared the area and blocked the road as we witnessed the devastation on TV reports.

I filled the gutters with water on Dad's roof and then did the same at Mum's house in Stonyfell where she had just moved the week before.

A week later I ran the fire track around the hills up to Mount

Osmond. Heat still radiated out like the earth was sending a message. Soon bright green tufts of grass broke through the soil and the regeneration began.

At the Mount we gather for a photo around a cake and talk about how Dad once won the inaugural Melbourne Vaughan Trophy. He smiles like he did almost forty years before. The look of an excited schoolboy who could hardly believe it.

'Upset a few people, that win did,' Dad says as we stare at the trophy cabinet.

He'd played off a handicap of 36.

We walk the clubhouse steps and look out onto the panoramic view of the city on a day without a cloud to be seen.

In the hours before Dad died, I sat at his wooden table on the balcony writing his eulogy. I thought about all those conversations sitting in the sunshine looking out over the Adelaide city skyline.

Dad passed away on the Sunday night not long after Ralph, Meredith and I sat by his bedside talking about old times. A few nights earlier I'd fed Dad ice-cream, the only food he could stomach. When Steve and Mum walked in, Dad pointed to them.

'Family,' he said.

For a moment Dad's eyes focused on me. He saw me clearly one last time and gave me this enormous grin while shaking my hand.

He was saying goodbye.

My old mates Paul, Mark, Gary, Greg and Sam come to the funeral. Brian and Heather who welcomed Les into their home all those years ago deliver hugs and handshakes. I read Dad's eulogy slowly and carefully, like I used to open the batting. I struggle at first but am able to get through it. Eventually I hit a few in the middle. He would have liked that.

Postscript

2019. What we thought was an ordinary visit to the optometrist for our ten-year-old son Harry turns into a nightmare.

My beautiful little boy, whose smile and laughter reminds me of striking a clean cover drive and watching it all the way to the boundary. Almost overnight he's been seeing what he describes as 'white blotches' in his eyes. A vision test reveals damage. We are told to take Harry to the Emergency Department immediately.

At the specialist's, the news is delivered that Harry has permanent damage to his macular. We are told there may be cerebral inflammation, and that our boy will get all the support he needs. It's most likely it's been there for a while and that Harry's brain was compensating to cope with the changes.

Harry is prescribed medication on a temporary basis in the hope it might work. His is such a rare condition, they just don't know.

It's too much for Harry. He breaks down in tears as we comfort him and try to absorb what we are being told. Harry is close to legally blind. We are told there are more questions to answer but the cause of the harm, from an autoimmune disease, is unknown.

We wait for six weeks. The time passes slowly. We meet with his teachers who listen carefully, and discreetly put in place measures to help him in the classroom.

Tempers fray. Understandably, on some days Harry's anger bubbles to the surface after school. I'm amazed at his bravery and ability to press ahead.

Then slowly, ever so slowly, there is a shift …

I watch Harry play soccer. He only has trouble when the ball is suddenly upon him. He moves confidently around the ground.

The night before the specialist appointment, Harry asks me to throw him a small rubber ball to dive into the pool to catch.

'Are you sure?'

'Throw it, Dad, I want to see how I go.'

To my surprise, he catches the ball with ease.

'Make them harder,' he excitedly yells.

The next day specialist's report comes in. There has been an unexpected improvement in his eyesight.

The medication appears to be working. His condition has stabilised. He still has some damage, but things are much better.

Weeks later, his MRI scan is clear.

He will need to be continually monitored and we don't know what the future holds.

We breathe again.

I cry as I write these words but not like before. As Greg Chappell learned – and as he helped me discover – in life there is always a second innings.

Acknowledgements

A massive thanks to Georgia Richter for her laser-sharp editing skills, and to Claire Miller, Chloe Walton and the crew at Fremantle Press for their investment in this project. Early on Glenn Morrison advised to me tell the story in alternating time frames, which proved invaluable. Mike Sexton provided encouragement and words of wisdom, as did Rob Bath whose idea it was to name the book *Second Innings*. Warwick Franks advised me if I ever became stuck to write 'one sentence at a time', a sentiment I've always remembered. Chris Hamilton has encouraged me in small but significant ways. Paul Twiss, Mark Clisby, Gary and Greg Slack were among several friends whose generosity knew no bounds when I visited Adelaide to see my parents during some of the period of the writing of this book. My cousin Chris Nicholls and his son Jake helped provide information about my paternal grandfather. My cousin Peter Blight was also a rich source of family history on my mother's side. Finally, thanks must go to my partner Ann for her support over many years and my kids, who continue to ask, 'What are you writing about now?'